I1062208

JOHN R. DEW, Ed.D.

Quality-Centered Strategic Planning

A STEP-BY-STEP GUIDE

QUALITY RESOURCES.

A Division of The Kraus Organization Limited
New York, New York

Most Quality Resources books are available at quantity discounts when purchased in bulk. For more information contact:

Special Sales Department
Quality Resources
A Division of the Kraus Organization Limited
902 Broadway
New York, New York 10010
800-247-8519

Copyright © 1997 John R. Dew, Ed.D.

All rights reserved. No part of this work covered by the copyrights hereon may be reproduced or used in any form or by any means — graphic, electronic, or mechanical, including photocopying, recording, taping, or information storage and retrieval systems — without written permission of the publisher.

Printed in the United States of America

01 00 99 98 97   10 9 8 7 6 5 4 3 2 1

Quality Resources
A Division of The Kraus Organization Limited
902 Broadway
New York, NY 10010
212-979-8600
800-247-8519

(∞) The paper used in this publication meets the minimum requirements of American National Standard for Information Sciences — Permanence of Paper for Printed Library Materials, ANSI Z39.48-1984.

ISBN 0-527-76308-X

Library of Congress Cataloging-in-Publication Data

Dew, John R.
    Quality-centered strategic planning : a step-by-step guide / John R. Dew.
        p.   cm.
    Includes bibliographical references and index.
    ISBN 0-527-76308-X (alk. paper)
    1. Strategic planning. 2. Total quality management. I. Title.
HD30.28.D484 1997
658.4'012—dc21   97-505
                                                            CIP

This book is dedicated to my mentors and to my wife, Lyndia.

Contents

Preface

This book offers ideas and specific recommendations directed toward the interests of three types of readers.

First, this book is for quality managers in for-profit companies, government agencies, and non-profit organizations. Quality managers have lead the revolution that has transformed American industry and government over the last decade, placing the United States in the forefront of world-class performance. This book provides quality managers with additional strategies and tactics to further the quality revolution within their specific organizations.

The second audience comprises the quality professionals who do not manage a quality program, but serve on the front lines of the quality revolution. These are the people who are called upon to implement an organization's quality program, and may be involved in facilitating a strategic planning process. This book provides facilitators with specific tools and techniques to enrich their current repertoire for addressing strategic issues.

The third audience for the work is the line managers who are seeking to improve their organizations in a practical way. It is my hope that line managers will embrace the philosophies advanced in this book and champion quality as the cornerstone of their organizations.

Quality professionals approach their work from a wide range of perspectives, drawing on many teachers, standards, and methodologies. Regardless of approach, the need to treat quality as a foundation for strategic planning runs true for all organizations. Many chapters in this work include specific notes referring to both the Malcolm Baldrige National Quality Award and the ISO 9000 series of quality standards, since these are widely used frameworks for quality programs. These notes link the key concepts of quality-centered strategic planning to broad reference points used within the quality profession.

Regardless of whether an organization is a small family-owned company, a city government, a multinational corporation, or even the government of a nation, its success depends on its ability to understand its mission, create an inspiring vision, develop objectives that will achieve the mission and vision, and create specific actions to accomplish the objectives. Throughout this process, quality must be ingrained as an essential ingredient in order to ensure success. If you agree with this observation and you seek to understand this process, this book is meant for you.

Author's Note

The examples in this book are real. They are drawn from my twenty-five years of experience in the quality field. I have worked with small and large city governments, colleges, precision machining operations, automotive plastic manufacturing, chemical processing, healthcare providers, legal offices, research scientists, nuclear reactor operations, law enforcement, analytical laboratories, aluminum smelting, water treatment facilities, and heavy industrial metal processing in the pursuit of quality improvement. The examples used are drawn from a wide range of experiences; from working with a stealth fighter pilot on Air Force TQM to comparing notes with undertakers, from training for workers on the space shuttle system to working with people who repair city streets.

Chapter 1

Quality and the Future

Operating the coal-fired steam plant at a research and development laboratory had never been considered a desirable job. But when the operators were challenged to define their mission and develop a strategic plan, they amazed everyone. While most people would think that the mission of a steam plant is to produce steam, the operators realized that their true mission was to provide comfort for the researchers. The operators wanted to run a system that performed so well the researchers would never have to think about whether it was too hot or too cold in their labs. The operators had a vision of their workplace that placed a high value on the quality of their work and the reliability of their equipment in order to please their customers.

A strategic planning team was created in a small city to apply for Federal Empowerment Zone status with the Housing and Urban Development Administration. As the team listened to citizens and reviewed the trends of the preceding decades, one issue became very clear: The quality of the community's low income housing had gradually declined and was now a major factor in the city's future. There were many causes for this situation, but the realization of the problem began to drive the planning process. For the community to achieve its strategic vision, a major effort had to be made to address the quality of homes and to fix the system that had allowed the quality to falter.

A small college faced a financial crisis. In order to rally support, the school's president formed a planning team, which included faculty, students, alumni, administrators, and trustees. They struggled over their vision for what the school should become and how to achieve that vision. One issue quickly became evident. The school would stand or fall based upon its reputation for delivering a high-quality liberal arts education in its region of the country. Quality became the principal factor in decision making and in communicating to potential donors and students.

A local affiliate of Habitat for Humanity had been building houses for over a decade. The officers gathered together for a strategic planning session in order to set the direction for the coming decade. There were many ideas about what to do and how to be more efficient. However, one issue stood out over all other factors. This affiliate had a reputation for building high-quality homes. The houses looked good and they were well built. This high standard for quality in construction became the focal point for all decisions to be made regarding the coming decade.

These are four real examples from business, government, education, and the volunteer sector. They all share the common theme of the need for a vision and a strategic plan that embraces quality as the foundation for an organization.

All organizations exist to provide some type of useful service. Some are established to earn a profit for their service, while others are established through government or voluntary agencies to provide services at cost. Regardless of whether an organization is a for-profit business, a non-profit organization, or a government agency, it will have a mission, a product or service that it provides, and customers who receive and/or pay for those services and products.

In the last decade there has been a great awakening among for-profit companies, non-profits, and in government that quality is an essential ingredient in the success of any organization. Dr. W. Edwards Deming admonished corporate leaders to improve their quality in order to lower costs, thereby capturing market share and sustaining long-term profitability. Managers in the public sector also heard Deming and set to work to build governmental services around the same principles.

The greatly increased quality consciousness raises a philosophical and a practical issue for all organizations.

- Is quality a means for achieving the organization's mission, or is quality an integral part of the mission itself?

- How should quality be integrated into the organization's overall strategic planning process?

This book is written from the perspective that the achievement of high quality constitutes an essential part of the mission for any organization and that a wide variety of strategies exist for achieving quality. To separate quality from the organization's core mission and purpose and to treat it as just a strategy is like saying that you will treat breathing as a strategy for living. You cannot live long without breathing, just as your organization cannot live long without a core emphasis on quality.

How your organization addresses the need for quality is open to strategy. The use of audits, statistical tools, cross-functional teams, and benchmarking are strategies that can be employed to provide a quality service to a customer.

Evolving Perceptions of Strategic Planning

The concept of having a strategic plan to implement an organization's quality process gained acceptance as a result of the Malcolm Baldrige National Quality Award. The team that established the original award criteria was wise in high-lighting this as an important aspect of an organization's quality program.

The Baldrige design team could probably tell from their own experiences that the lack of a strategic vision and plan would leave an organization adrift—implementing their efforts without a means to anchor them to the core interests of the organization.

Dr. Joseph Juran has been a driving force behind the advancement of ideas about senior-level management's responsibility to plan and manage quality just as they do an organization's financial plan. Juran's work on leadership suggested that a strong focus on quality should become a core responsibility for any organization that wanted to survive.

Should an organization develop a strategic plan for operating the business and a separate plan for addressing the initiatives needed to achieve high quality? A decade ago the answer would have been yes, since most organizations' strategic plans ignored the quality imperative. A separate strategic quality plan was much better than having no plan dealing with quality at all.

Today, the answer should be *no*. Quality is too important to be a secondary plan. Quality is the *sine qua non*, that which one cannot do without, for all organizations. Therefore, what organizations need today is a process for strategic thinking and planning that embraces quality as the organization's core value. Organizations that will survive will be those that have a strategic plan that frames other issues, such as finances, human resources, and facilities from within the context of achieving quality.

This broader understanding of the foundational role of quality in formulating strategy led to changes in the Baldrige Award in 1996. The original term, "strategic quality planning," has been replaced with the general term "strategic planning" to indicate a blending of quality into the core of the organization's philosophy and actions. The phrase "quality-centered strategic planning" refines and sharpens the focus of the concept of integrating quality into the strategic planning process.

In the same manner, ISO 9000 does not call for strategic planning but implies that the quality policy and quality management system will be integrated into the fabric of thinking, decision making, and strategic planning in each organization.

Operational Definitions

For the purposes of this book, an organization's mission is to provide high-quality service to a customer. The organization can be established to render a profit or not make a profit in the course of fulfilling its mission.

All organizations have objectives that are major goals that must be achieved in order to accomplish the mission. Enabling actions are the strategies and tactics that an organization uses to achieve its objectives.

For example, an organization's mission may be to provide high-quality healthcare services. An objective that supports the mission can be to always provide the right medication to the right patient. An enabling action will be to have a quality control program and audits to assure that the objective is achieved, in support of the mission. Specific quality tools, such as audits or control charts, are enabling actions, or can be thought of as a means to an end.

A strategic plan is a planning document, developed through a specific process (to be described in this book), that orients an organization toward its mission by placing its central focus on the objectives and enabling actions that impact quality—the very life-source of the organization.

How Does Your Organization Envision the Future?

How we think about the future has a great influence on our willingness to engage in strategic planning. How we think about quality influences whether it is the founding principle of our organization. So, before exploring the process of strategic planning, it is useful to reflect on how people in your organization think about quality and the future.

How do the leaders in your organization think about the future? Is it something that is going to happen next week, next quarter, or perhaps next year? Do your organization's leaders think about the future in terms of a few years from now? Perhaps the future is what comes after the next election. Perhaps your organization sees the future as seven or ten years away, or even decades away.

Do leaders in your organization know the history of your group and understand how the historical events have created the situation you now consider to be the present? Do they see the present as something that was caused to happen, or do they seem to think that the present state of things just kind of appeared one day while no one was paying much attention? In other words, how much influence do the leaders in your organization think they have over the events of the future?

The answers to these questions can tell you a lot about the level of understanding of the future in your organization. How your organization's leadership views the future influences the ability of your organization to create a strategy to influence its future. This perception of the future is rarely a formalized statement. Instead, it is usually an informal and often unarticulated sense.

It really does not matter what kind of organization you work in. You may be working in a factory, a financial institution, a medical facility, government, research, law enforcement, or a church. The similarities of these organizations far outweigh their distinguishing characteristics. The same question is still important in any organizational setting: How does your organization think about the future, and how does that impact its ability to influence the future through strategic planning?

Future Thoughts

We can envision a continuum of approaches to thinking about the future. This continuum runs from being totally numb to the future on one extreme, to being proactively involved. Between these extremes are various levels of awareness and control over the future. Figure 1.1 shows an example of this continuum.

Figure 1.1. Styles of Thinking About the Future

Numb	Reactive	Proactive
We can't influence it. It's coming too fast.	We're ready for next week. We're ready for next year.	We influence what's coming.

People think in different ways along this continuum for many different reasons. What is important is to break out of the numbness and reactive thinking and grasp the essential notion that the organization is what people make of it. The future is what people want it to become.

Of course there are unexpected things that happen to individuals and organizations. But even adverse setbacks may be anticipated and their effect minimized. A community that plans for a flood can sustain a lot less damage than a community that has no plan.

How Does Your Organization Relate to Quality?

There are many definitions for quality and many ways to think about it. Quality is like a diamond that has many facets when held up to the light. Quality can mean one thing to a customer and something else to a person making a product. People in the education field may view quality as something quite different from people working in a factory. All of these perspectives are valid, but the organization's point of view about quality will influence the manner in which it relates to the strategic planning process.

There are five basic ways to look at the quality issue. Three of them will make quality unimportant in the organization's strategic vision, and two will treat quality as an essential ingredient.

Figure 1.2. Continuum of Perceptions About Quality

Conformance to requirements	Assurance and control	Intangible essence
Corrective actions	Continuous improvement	

1. Quality as Conformance to Requirements

The first approach to quality is to define it as conformance to a set of requirements. This perspective sees quality as a measurement of whether or not requirements are met. If all the requirements are met, there are zero defects and it follows that there will be adequate quality in the job at hand. There are merits to this point of view. With this approach, quality can be quantified and the cost of obtaining it can be determined. Likewise, the attributes that cause poor quality can be identified and the cost of poor quality can be measured. Viewing quality as conformance to requirements can be an effective enabling action for many organizations.

However, viewing quality as conformance to requirements often places quality outside the area of strategic planning; it is a reactive way of thinking which does not propel quality into the decision-making process of the organization. At its worst, this approach creates a mindset in which people think of quality as something that must be done to stay out of trouble. At its best, this view encourages people to think of quality as an important ingredient in containing costs and keeping customers from complaining.

People working in high-risk businesses, such as flying airplanes or operating nuclear power reactors, may indeed view total compliance and zero defects as a key strategic issue. They are clear exceptions to the general observation that viewing quality as conforming to requirements restricts the ability to treat quality as a strategic issue for the organization.

2. Quality as Corrective Actions

A second reactive approach is to perceive quality as taking corrective actions to fix things that go wrong. In many organizations, the quality function only gets involved when there is a problem. Hospitals, for instance, used to consider the quality assurance function to only be one of diagnosing the cause of death of a patient. Did the patient die from the disease, the actions of the doctor, or something the hospital did?

Corrective actions are a necessary part of a quality program if proactive design and control actions prove ineffective. There is a great problem in considering corrective actions to be the core of a quality philosophy. This approach is wholly reactive and does not move quality into any part of the planning process other than to fix what went wrong from previous mistakes. It is a vicious cycle. Unfortunately for many organizations, the concept of quality is linked solely with auditing and taking corrective actions. While auditing is a valuable quality tool, a quality philosophy based primarily on auditing and corrective actions creates a policing function that is essentially reactive.

3. Quality as Anticipating and Preventing Problems

A third approach to defining quality is to see it as a process for planning and taking actions that anticipate and prevent problems. This view encompasses much of the discipline of quality assurance and quality control, and again can serve as a valuable enabling action within organizations.

In quality assurance, planners take a systematic approach to the design, fabrication, operation, and even decommissioning of a process. Checks and balances are carefully employed to ensure that potential problems are identified and avoided. The quality of the manufacturing or service system is assured through systematic efforts. For example, an engineering design document can be required to be reviewed independently by another engineer to ensure that an error is not made.

In quality control, the important quality attributes of a process are defined. A systematic method is developed to measure these quality attributes in order to obtain high-quality output from the process. For example, the dimensions of a machine part are defined, along with tolerances, and measurements are made to assess the variation in the machining process and the acceptance of the parts.

Quality assurance and quality control are ways of conceptualizing quality as an important tool for the organization along with other important tools, such as finance, marketing, public relations, and human resources.

4. Quality as Continuous Improvement

A fourth, more proactive approach is to frame quality as a basis for continuous improvement in an organization. With this approach, every system in the organization is ripe for improvement. There is a constant challenge to remove errors and rework, and then to use other methods, such as cycle time reduction and reengineering, to achieve breakthroughs in performance. For example, many organizations now expect teams of employees to study their work processes and constantly seek ways to improve those processes.

Using quality as a process of continuous improvement can be accomplished in both small steps and bold leaps forward. Juran originated the concept of quality as continuous improvement, in which teams and individuals focus on specific opportunities and, through diagnosis, bring about a breakthrough. This is like hitting lots of singles to win a ballgame. At the same time, some batters can hit home runs, so the organization needs to look for the occasional major effort that can dramatically improve performance. The current interest in business process reengineering is the organizational equivalent of hitting home runs. In the American culture home runs are more valued, even though a team with lots of singles might actually win the game.

The concept of quality as a process of continuous improvement aligns the quality function with the strategic planning process. Rather than reacting to situations, continuous quality improvement will help the organization shape its destiny. Continuous improvement positions the quality function in a role to better influence the future of the organization.

5. Quality as Intangible

In many settings quality is perceived in a fifth manner. Rather than being just a quantifiable ingredient, quality is also thought of as an intangible essence. While quality professionals might rightly argue that the attributes of the essence of quality can be traced back to quantifiable actions, the people who hold to this view will see quality as being a standard of excellence which is difficult to define. "I can't define it, but I know it when I see it," is the philosophy of many service organizations, and it is a valid point of view in many cases.

This perception of quality as an intangible essence can impact the strategic planning of the organization. In the example of the small college in the opening of this chapter, it might indeed have been possible to measure the number of volumes in the library, the number of professors with doctorates, and the student/professor ratio, but all of those values would not have captured the flavor of excellence in a small college. The intangible quality of the educational process defined what the future course of the institution would be when possible options were considered.

It is well established that some people think in a "left-brain" manner and some think in a "right-brain" manner. Left-brain thinking gathers specific facts and forms a perception based on the evidence. Right-brain thinking captures situations in a holistic manner—often leading to an intuitive grasp of the situation. Envisioning quality as an intangible essence is a completely right-brain phenomenon. Readers who are left-brain thinkers can feel free to dismiss this view completely. Right-brain thinkers who read this will know exactly what this point is about.

Quality as an intangible essence often means there is an unquantifiable spirit or commitment to excellence in an organization—an *esprit de corps*. There really is a social reality known as team spirit, but it is difficult to quantify because the act of measuring it changes it.

Quality and Strategic Planning

There is a dynamic link between how people envision the future and how they perceive quality as a vital force in creating the strategic direction of the organization.

Figure 1.3 illustrates this relationship using a graph that provides a vertical axis for the reactive to proactive views regarding quality, and a horizontal axis for the continuum from reactive to proactive thinking about the future.

Figure 1.3.   Perception of Quality and the Future

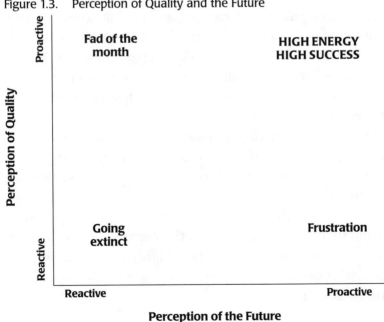

This graphs shows us that when an organization has a proactive view of quality but lacks proactive perceptions of the future, the organization will be stuck in a cycle of introducing one new fad after another. The latest book, the latest tool, the word from the most recent conference will be tried, but with little results.

A reactive approach to quality combined with a proactive perception of the future offers a formula for frustration. The people in the organization want to move out and take the lead in their market niche, but their every effort is stymied by some problem that was not anticipated. Just when the organization seems to be picking up speed for change, some new crisis comes along and robs the momentum. The organization has great planning but spends all its time putting out fires.

A combination of reactive views on quality and the future spells extinction for any organization. Such an organization will fall behind its proactive competitors. The American view of passenger trains offers a good illustration. Companies that were not willing to improve upon the quality of their train services grew fatalistic about their future and maintained the status quo. Train services in other countries, which constantly improved, rose above their competitors due to proactive planning.

The dynamic organization that can thrill its customers and capture the market share is the organization that combines a proactive approach to quality with proactive thinking about the future.

The combination of strategic planning and a proactive quality program is the organizational equivalent of a fission reaction. Two highly potent masses are placed together to unleash a vast amount of organizational power.

Why Emphasize Quality-Centered Strategic Planning?

In any organization, a well-balanced quality philosophy and program will address many issues. This point is illustrated by the various evaluation criteria in the Malcolm Baldrige National Quality Award.

The award criteria were established in 1988 with input from quality leaders in manufacturing and service organizations, the academic community, and consultants. As a method for evaluating quality programs, it covers the predictable areas of statistical process control, effective utilization of human resources, and the methods for quality improvement that have been championed by Joseph Juran.

Strategic planning is one of the seven major evaluation criteria for this award. This addresses not only the planning of the quality process in an organization, but the manner in which quality serves as a key element in the organization's overall strategic plan.

Regardless of which standard one uses to measure the effectiveness of quality programs, be it the Baldrige Award, ISO 9000, or the Nuclear Quality Assurance-1 standard, quality must be planned into the fabric of the organization if it is to succeed. There is likewise fairly universal agreement among the quality experts that effective organizations will wrap quality into their strategic planning process as a vital element. When quality is left as an afterthought, it cannot be effectively built into the organization. The strategic plan must be built around quality planning.

This point can be illustrated by looking at three companies that have won the Baldrige Award. For example, at Cadillac Motor Car Company, "the business plan is the quality plan and the business planning process is focused on continuously improving the quality of Cadillac products, processes, and services."[1] At the Wallace Company, senior leadership develops annual quality strategic objectives that drive the quality process.[2] At AT&T Universal Card Services the organization integrated their total quality management objectives into their strategic and business plans. According to AT&T, "our planning process is driven by our vision, values, and culture, and allows us to maneuver rapidly and effectively in a dynamic business environment."[3]

When an organization does not respect quality as a strategic principle, it will fail. The best example is the failure of the quality circle movement. There was nothing wrong with having quality circles, and some excellent training procedures were developed to support them. However, when the attempt was made to graft quality circles onto existing structures that did not fundamentally value quality, the endeavor always failed. Unless an organization came to accept quality as a fundamental factor in success or failure, the quality circle was doomed to be a passing fad.[4]

Many excellent people have burned out as they sought to bring the quality revolution to their organizations. The organization did not embrace quality as a fundamental value; therefore the efforts to bring it in the back door were always going to meet with limited success until a fundamental breakthrough in thinking could occur. It has taken much effort within many organizations to bring us to the current

---

1. Cadillac Motor Car Company, *Cadillac: The Quality Story,* Detroit, Michigan (1991).

2. *Wallace Co., Inc. 1990 Malcolm Baldrige National Quality Award Winner: A Condensed Version of the Company's Application for the Award.* American Productivity & Quality Center (1991).

3. "A Summary of the AT&T Universal Card Services Malcolm Baldrige National Quality Award Application," *Proceedings of the Quality and Productivity Management Association's Spring 1993 Conference* QPMA (1993).

4. Stephen J. Holoviak, "Negative Attitudes and Quality Circles," *Quality Digest* (April 1989), 79–83.

level of appreciation of quality. There is still a long way to go as organizations begin to obtain higher levels of energy by integrating quality into the core of the strategic planning process.

Quality as a Core Value

A few years ago I was leading a seminar on quality improvement in Las Vegas. A group of serious-looking men in dark suits filled the front row. They would whisper to each other and exchange silent looks of understanding. "Who are these guys?" I kept asking myself. During a break, I found out that they were all managers from the largest mortuary firm in Nevada and they were dead serious about quality. "Hey, it's a process," they told me. "It's a repeat business, too. The same families will come back for our services and quality is important."

In almost any endeavor, quality can become a core value that defines an organization and sets the expectations for performance. For a community, the issue may be the quality of living. For a business, it may be the quality of products or services, or of work life within the organization. In education, quality may center around many different factors, such as the mentoring of teachers and the state of classrooms and laboratories for imparting state-of-the-art knowledge. In healthcare, quality can focus on the correct diagnosis and treatment of an illness. Quality is a key factor for non-profit organizations in their ability to achieve their mission.

In each case, there is a process for achieving a synthesis of strategic planning and quality. While people often have an intuitive grasp of the importance of quality in the goals of an organization, there are steps that can be taken to bring quality into clear focus. This will enhance the organization's ability to create the high-quality future that the leaders, customers, and members of the organization seek.

A Strategic Planning Process

Several broad steps comprise the process for strategic planning for any organization:

1. Listen to the customers' needs.
2. Plan how you will meet the customers' needs.
3. Be aware of your values and align your organization to serve the customers.
4. Be aware of the forces that will influence you.
5. Develop specific quality objectives.
6. Consider various scenarios.
7. Plan to close the gaps.
8. Take actions to achieve the objectives.
9. Reevaluate and renew effort.

Strategic planning begins with the customer in mind. The questions to ask revolve around who the organization's customers will be, what they will want, and what trends will impact them during the coming years.

After the planners have considered the customers' perspective, they must next determine where the organization should be in relation to the customers. An organization must designate people to prepare a plan. These planners can be identified in a variety of ways, as detailed in the latter part of this Chapter. Should the organization keep the same customers? Expand into new customer areas? Give up, maintain, or expand market positions? Quality should be a major factor in reaching decisions regarding positioning the organization with its customers. A successful organization will focus its energies on its areas of excellence, where it provides high-quality service and products to customers in the most profitable manner. Weak areas, such as endeavors where quality is low, scrap costs are high, or customers have complaints, must either be targeted for change or abandoned as untenable.

When the planners have clarified their vision regarding how to position the organization with its customers, the next step is to work on the internal vision. The form of the organization may need to change in order to achieve the desired outcome.

As the planners anticipate the customers' needs, plan the organization's position with the customers, and plan the internal changes to achieve the vision, they must also attend to the broad horizon of trends and future conditions that will impact the organization. Depending upon the mission of the organization, there will be demographic studies, long-term economic forecasts, and technical projections to help assess the future. A quick review of the history of an organization also does a great deal to help discern what the future may hold.

Once the planners embrace a vision of what the organization will become, it is imperative to identify the main gaps between where the organization is and where it wants to be. In a specific manner, the planners should note the key steps to be taken to achieve the vision.

With the important gaps clearly identified, the planners must take steps to close the gaps between the vision and the current reality. This is often the hardest part of the planning process. There are many day-to-day forces that will divert attention and resources from enacting the strategic plan. Ingrained behaviors must be resisted in order to take new steps toward achieving the vision.

Implementing the steps in the plan means taking action and assessing the effectiveness of the action. There will undoubtedly be resistance to any change that must be overcome. There must also be a periodic reassessment of the strategic plan to ensure that the vision is still accurate and to

Figure 1.4. Strategic Planning Cycle

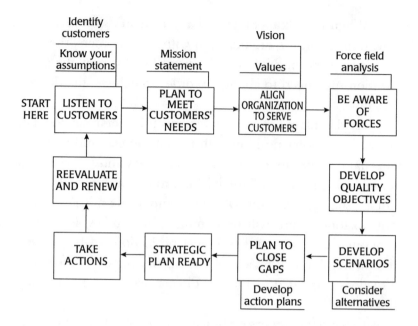

determine the amount of progress being made in closing the gaps. The strategic planning process becomes a cyclical process within the organization (see Figure 1.4).

There are many steps in this cycle; this book will examine each in some detail. This can create the false impression that the execution of each step, and the overall process, are time consuming. The actual planning process can move quickly, as described in Chapter 10. After examining the chapters that detail the steps in the strategic planning process, it is important to look at how you can "blitz-build" your plan, in order to see how it fits together in a timely manner.

This is a lot like learning Tai Chi. First you learn the forms, then you learn the flow. First, we examine the specific tools and steps along the way, then we put it all together so it will flow smoothly.

Involving People in the Process

I have a vision that I want you to implement. Does that inspire you to cooperate with me? Certainly not. However, if you help create the goals or vision for this year, you may be more likely to support their implementation.

The strategic planning process needs to involve as many people in the organization as possible. Can this be done for a small organization? Without a doubt. How about large organizations? Where you cannot involve everyone, then make sure that everyone's interests are represented by someone who is trusted and respected.

In a large business, all of the stakeholders need to be represented in the strategic planning process. This means that management and the employees must work together. It means getting people from the various departments involved. It often means encouraging groups of stakeholders to share their input throughout the planning effort and to review proposed plans.

Create a Strategic Planning Team

The management of the organization must initiate the strategic planning process and make sure that it continues. While management is responsible for making the planning process work, the actual planning is best carried out by a team. The team should consist of a diagonal cross-section of people in the organization to ensure that all interests are being met (see Figure 1.5).

In addition, a team consisting of a diagonal cross-section of the employees provides the best information about what is really going on in the organization. A planning team that consists of only senior-level managers runs a high risk that vital information and perspectives will be filtered out and be absent from the planning process. Using a diagonal cross-section ensures that information from middle levels and those who perform hands-on work, or have direct contact with customers, will be able to share their valuable knowledge. At the same time, the team will have senior-level people who are able to provide a broad view of the organization's situation. For example, the Cadillac Quality Council is not just a management-driven group. The council is co-chaired by an international representative of the United Auto Workers and involves people from a broad set of perspectives. In the government sector, we can look at the quality council in the city of Saint Paul. This group includes representatives from management and unions, with many members who are front-line employees in city service organizations.

It is very important to have all of these perspectives included in developing a strategic plan. Juran and Deming have clearly diagnosed the problems of developing a quality effort without senior management. The middle managers, who translate budgets into actions, must be involved in the process to ensure that the plan can be implemented. Those who have direct contact with the product, the processes, and the customers also need to be involved to give the plan meaning.

In small organizations it may be possible to get everybody in one room together at the same time. A facilitator can lead the process and aim for total involvement and commitment from the whole group.

Figure 1.5.   Create a Strategic Planning Team that Is a Diagonal Slice of the Organization

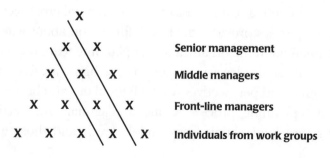

In a city, the residents need to be involved in focus groups and in reviewing plans. Elected leaders, along with community leaders and grass-roots leaders all need to participate in the planning process. A plan developed exclusively by the planners will have no validity, even though it may be an excellent plan on paper.

In large businesses, the planning team needs to include senior and middle management, front-line supervision, and people who work directly on production or with customers. If the organization has a union, then the union leaders should be invited to participate in the process as well.

In social service organizations, the managers and service providers need to be involved along with people who can speak for the service recipients: the customers.

Figure 1.6. Strategic Planning Roles and Actions

Step	People Involved	Actions
Listen to customers	Create a strategic planning team*	Customers identified internal assumptions understood
Plan to meet customers' needs	Strategic planning team	Mission statement prepared with strong quality focus
Align organization to serve customers	Strategic planning team	Vision statement values clarification
Be aware of forces	Strategic planning team	Force field analysis
Develop quality objectives	Strategic planning team	Identify key objectives and enabling objectives
Develop scenarios	Strategic planning team, line and staff groups	Consider alternatives
Plan to close gaps	Line managers, strategic planning team reviews	Develop action plans
Take actions	Line management leads	Line and staff groups implement plans
Reevaluate and renew	Senior management brings strategic planning team back together	• Review mission or vision • Check status of actions • Refine key objectives and enabling objectives

*The strategic planning team includes the organization's senior management and a diagonal slice of the organization.

In a school, the administrators and teachers need to be involved, but so do the students. In many cases, it is advisable to include trustees, alumni, or elected officials in the strategic planning team.

Attention must always be given to ensure that a planning team is diverse, within the context of the organization. An effective team will have a balance of perspectives from within and without the organization. It is important to have a balance of perspectives from men and women, from newcomers and established members of the community or workplace, from different racial or ethnic backgrounds, and from a variety of age groups. The quality of the planning process is enhanced by the diversity of the planning group. The validity of the plan is likewise strengthened by the assurance that all perspectives are involved in the creative process.

The Quality Manager's Role

While the senior-level managers of an organization are responsible for achieving the organization's mission—and thereby its standards for quality—many organizations now employ quality managers.

The role of the quality manager varies greatly from one organization to the next. In successful organizations, the quality manager works closely with other senior-level managers and serves as a vocal proponent for quality. The quality manager should be a key player in the organization's strategic planning by championing the strategic planning process.

There are many examples of successful organizations in which the quality manager plays a strong role as quality advocate among the senior managers. The Ritz-Carlton Hotel Company (a 1992 Baldrige Award winner) has a vice-president of quality who drives the quality emphasis. Xerox Corporation (a 1989 Baldrige winner) has a director of corporate quality who champions the "Xerox 2000, Leadership Through Quality" program. IBM Rochester (a 1990 Baldrige winner) has a director of market-driven quality who leads the company in its efforts to be customer-driven.[5]

This person must get beyond the numerous roadblocks and initiate the process. Chapter 9 provides a detailed discussion of possible obstacles and offers actions that can be taken to overcome them.

Once the quality manager has obtained agreement to initiate a strategic planning process, he or she must assemble the right mix of people to form a planning team. The quality manager must have agreement from other managers that the team members will be given adequate time to work on this process.

The quality manager will either facilitate the process or ensure that it is led by an experienced facilitator. Often, the quality manager needs to participate as a team member, so it is advisable to utilize a facilitator who is neutral regarding the plan's content and who will focus on the planning process. If a skilled facilitator is not available inside the organization, the quality manager can often find experienced facilitators through the local chapter of the American Society for Quality Control. In some communities, the Chamber of Commerce will have access to people who can facilitate the planning process. Many community colleges and regional universities have faculty members who can also provide neutral facilitation for the organization.

Quality managers are often far ahead of their organizations in recognizing the need for a proactive view of quality as a cornerstone of the organization. Because quality managers attend quality conferences, read quality books, and attend meetings for quality professionals, they may become frustrated

---

5. Frank Cap, "The Continuing Quest for Excellence," *Quality Progress* vol. 28, number 12 (December 1995).

by the rate of progress within their own organizations. It is very easy for the quality manager to be seen as overly zealous by the rest of the management.

The participative process of developing a strategic plan provides the quality manager with an excellent mechanism to bring the rest of the key managers up to speed. While the quality manager sponsors the process, the line managers develop an ownership of the content. This process helps the quality manager avoid being isolated from his or her organization over time and provides a new leverage for making gains in the quality program to support the health of the organization.

Getting Started

If you are a senior manager reading this book, you should be thinking about how to integrate quality into your organization's mission. Now you have the opportunity to integrate quality and strategic planning in a holistic manner. You can lead your organization toward an integrated goal and bring your people in out of the wilderness of management fads.

If you are a quality manager reading this book, you may have appreciated the various perspectives of the future and approaches to integrating quality, but you are probably ready to go into more detail. Just remember, what requires a chapter of discussion in this book may often be accomplished in just an hour in group process with a good facilitator.

If you are reading this book as a front-line quality trooper, you may be called on to facilitate or participate in this overall process. I suggest you skim the whole book quickly and then come back and read over the areas that may be new to you, or that offer a different twist. As a potential strategic planning facilitator, it is important that you understand the tools, the theory behind the tools, and the overall flow of the planning process in order to be successful.

Baldrige and ISO 9000 Notes

The nine-step process examined in this book will provide a thorough quality-centered strategic plan for those who use the Baldrige Award criteria to guide their organization's efforts.

The award seeks to ensure that an organization has an efficient and effective process for developing a strategic plan. This process should have a special emphasis on listening to the customer, surveying the competitive environment, considering the organization's internal issues and capabilities, and determining the possibilities of establishing strategic partnerships. Once a plan is developed, the award assesses how the plan is translated into action with "actionable key business drivers."

As shown in Figure 1.4, quality-centered strategic planning is a cyclical process. Part of the award criteria addresses whether an organization works on improving its strategic planning process. (See Chapter 10 for some ideas on doing this.)

The award also evaluates how an organization deploys its strategic plan. How do actionable key business drivers flow down to work units in action plans? How are the quality improvement tools employed in implementing the strategic plan? And how does the organization establish performance indicators to measure the degree of success of implementing the plan?

Each of these issues is covered in specific examples and methods in this book.

ISO 9000 describes management responsibilities that will ensure that quality is addressed as a key strategic issue, including the establishment of a policy and a system that both include quality planning. The planning process in this book ensures that an organization basing its quality program on ISO 9000 has a management philosophy that serves the organization's central themes for short- and long-term planning.

Chapter 2

Begin with the Customer in Mind

The vice-president of a telecommunications company stood in the conference room at a customer's manufacturing plant. He had just shown a videotape to the plant's managers that described new developments in wireless telephone technology. "What I want to know from you," he said, "is how it would help you operate this plant if all your employees could be in touch by phone with this new wireless capability?" The implications of the technology were obvious to the managers as they considered the communication problems throughout their sprawling 2,000-acre facility.

The city's planning manager stood before a small gathering of citizens from an economically depressed part of town. This focus group had been called together to present ideas regarding what the people in the community wanted changed to improve the quality of their lives. People spoke about problems with drug dealers and difficulty in getting to and from work. Abandoned houses and insufficient recreational areas were discussed, along with the need for community support for the police. It was clear to everyone in the group that before the city started making plans for "helping" the community, the people in the community were going to be involved in defining the needs.

A department head from a community college sat in the office of a corporation's training manager. The college representative had made this appointment to find out what type of educational services were needed by this local company. They discussed the need for technical writing skills and basic literacy programs. They looked at options for offering evening classes that would appeal to the company's needs and be convenient for the employees. The training manager was delighted that the community college was willing to listen to the local needs and develop programs based on those needs.

A hospital administrator listened to the comments from a focus group of community leaders, doctors, and neighborhood representatives. Everyone shared the same concern about the need to provide low-cost, quick service for minor medical needs that were currently clogging up the emergency rooms. The administrator took this insight from her medical partners and clients and began to form a plan for establishing a free clinic in the local neighborhood to meet this need.

Each of these real examples illustrates the principle that to be successful in providing a service or making a product, we must begin with the customer in mind. What does the customer want? What does the customer need? How would the customer prefer the product to look? When would the customer prefer to receive this product or service?

The first step for the strategic planning team is to work on understanding the customers' needs. This means knowing who the customers are and understanding their current as well as their future needs.

Do not expect the customers to volunteer what they want. The customers' needs are constantly changing, just as your needs also evolve over time. As circumstances change, needs change as well. The organization that constantly listens to its customers will be able to recognize changing needs and position itself to meet those needs. In order to listen to the customer, the team must engage the customer in dialogue.

Customers often have needs and desires which they are not able to articulate, so the planning team must be assertive or proactive in seeking out the customers' opinions. In his lectures at George Washington University, Deming asserted that the customer's expectations are always set by what the supplier can envision and produce. No one cared about having pneumatic tires until Harvey Firestone started making them. When organizations wait until needs are fully articulated, then the strategic opportunity to be the first to offer a high-quality product or service has been lost. The team must learn to listen with a customer's ears, see with his eyes, and walk in his shoes.

Figure 2.1.   Listen to Your Customers

What	Why	How
Find out what your customer wants.	Success depends on meeting your customers' needs.	Identify your customer.
What is important to him or her.		Create the listening moment.
Clarify who your customers really are.		

How to Walk in Your Customers' Shoes

How can your planning team discover your customers' needs and identify the needs that the customers themselves might not even recognize? There are two things the quality manager must do to help the team. First, help the members recognize that there are things about your organization's perspective that are different from that of your customers. For instance, if you are managing a company, a city or county agency, or a school, you have a certain amount of knowledge about your field, a certain income level, and an expectation of how things are done in your organization. Yet, your customers may be much younger or older than you and may not have your income level. They probably have different ways of making decisions than you are used to in your organization. You may live in the Snow Belt and have customers in the sunny South. You may be located in the East, trying to serve customers in the Mountain States.

The planning team members must not project their own self-images onto their customers. The customers may share many core values with your organization, but they have their own unique aspects that your planning team needs to consider. It is legend how Detroit auto executives, living in the Mid-West, missed the importance of the growing number of imported cars on the West Coast! The planning team must be careful not to allow their own world view to filter out the view of their customers.

To listen to the customers you must get out of your frame of reference and go where *they* are. Go visit their offices, factories, schoolrooms, parks, and neighborhoods. You cannot listen to someone when you are too far away to hear what they have to say.

Identifying the Customer

Who are your customers? This is a tricky question for many organizations, and the planning team must start here. It is tricky because we often fail to recognize that there are two broad groups of customers. One group is the individuals or organizations who pay for a product or service. Because they are paying for a product or service, they get upset when their expectations are not met. The other group of customers includes the people who receive or use a product or service for which they have not personally paid. They may not see themselves as customers, but they are.

Who is the customer of a military contractor? Certainly the military organization that pays for the product or service. But the soldier or sailor who uses the product or service is just as much a customer.

Who is the customer of a college? The parents who pay the tuition, since they are paying for a service to be rendered. But the students are as well, since they make use of the educational services, even if they themselves are not paying the bill.

The customers of a social service agency are, of course, the taxpayers who pay for the agency's services, even if they do not make direct personal use of them. Their investment is like that of an endowment to a college. But the people who use the social service are customers as well, even though they may not financially support the agency. Like the soldier or the student, the person who receives food stamps or counseling is a customer by virtue of making use of the system. Service providers must be careful not to allow the service recipients to be seen as merely clients or patients—concepts that create distance and tend to objectify the service recipients. Service providers must remember that all clients and patients are customers too.

This broad definition of the concept of customer is essential for success in strategic planning. To restrict the definition of customer only to those who pay will lead to failure of the process in the majority of settings where it can be used.

It is often the perceptions of the non-paying customers—the students or the people who receive a social service—that hold the key to improving the organization's strategic focus and overall quality. Many organizations exist for the purpose of helping these non-paying customers, yet neglect them in the planning process. Ask the students about the textbooks, the classrooms. Ask the battered spouse about the quality of the spouse abuse program, then use that information in the planning process. Defense contractors need to talk with the soldiers in the field. Auto makers need to talk to the teenagers who will become new drivers.

The strategic planning team must spend time on this issue by jumping in and listening to the customers. It is essential to know *who* to listen to first. The quality manager will need to help the team in recognizing who all the customers are and should make sure that this step is accomplished up front. It is also helpful for the team to recognize some factors that may keep it from listening as well.

Identification of customers can be accomplished in two ways, depending on whether the organization is for-profit or not-for-profit. In for-profit settings, bring in the salespeople to learn who the customers are. Your sales manager will know who buys your product or service, how much they buy, and why they buy it. Your sales manager will also know who might buy your product or services but presently does not. If your business is too small to have a sales manager, then start compiling your list of customers when they call or walk in to make a purchase.

For non-profits, the process can be more complicated. Start by listing the funding agencies and individual donors who are stakeholders. Then add the names of the clients and beneficiaries who are another form of customer. Then choose from the listening methods listed in this chapter to discover what the voice of the customer is saying.

> Example: In developing a strategic plan for the Health Care Financing Administration, planners conducted focus group interviews with groups of Medicare beneficiaries (customers) to understand how these people defined and judged the quality of the health-care they receive. Prioritization of the customer's perspective should be determined by the customer, not the field researcher. In effective field research, the participants are asked how *they* would prioritize their needs and opinions.

What Keeps Us from Listening?

People who should be listening to their customers often fail to do so for a variety of reasons. The most obvious reason is that they do not recognize the need to listen. Things are okay now, so why rock the boat? True, going out and listening to customers can be hard work. It takes energy and effort to find out what the customers think.

In some cases we fail to listen to customers because we do not value their opinions. We believe we know more about their needs and our products and services than they do, so why listen to them?

In other cases, we deny what we hear from our customers because their opinions disturb what we believe to be true. No one will want to buy those small cars when we can make good big cars.

Once the planning team begins to listen to the customers, there are still some suppositions that might influence thinking about the future and the ability to effectively respond to what the customers want. One set of barriers is posed by the assumptions people have about the future, and another set relates to our lack of understanding of how technology travels and impacts a society.

Most people tend to fall into one of two camps regarding their unstated view of the future. People tend to either adopt a view based upon an assumption of limited resources, or one based upon an assumption that technology can overcome most problems (see Figure 2.2). Each side has a certain appeal and can utilize an abundance of examples to support its case. Either assumption will impact the manner in which the customer is perceived and heard.

The success of strategic planning depends on clearly hearing and understanding the customers. Filtering the customers' message through our own assumptions clouds our vision. For example, if I am in the business community, and I believe there is a limit to growth, I may not listen to my customer's expression of desire for more or better technology. I may tend to think that the customer should be happy with what he has and should stop wanting more.

On the other hand, I might be more attuned to what the customer is saying because the customer's needs and my concerns are well aligned. I may be able to interpret a customer's need for a better product as an opportunity to use recycled materials or remove a waste stream out of a process, for a win-win opportunity. Your assumptions about the current state of things and the future are going to influence how you listen to your customer. This is not necessarily bad or good; it could be either, depending on the circumstances. However, being aware of your own filters can enable you to become a better listener to the voice of your customer.

With a general belief in technical growth and expanding wealth, one might interpret the customer's voice from a point of view of technological fixes. The need to address crime might be interpreted as a need for high-technology prisons or the redistribution of the shortage of resources. The need to address inadequate housing might be interpreted as the need to build large, efficient housing complexes or as a matter of taxing those with expensive homes to provide resources for other people's housing.

Our perception of what the customer wants is often molded by our beliefs about the world around us. To listen to our customers and effectively develop a quality-centered

Figure 2.2.   Understanding Customer Needs

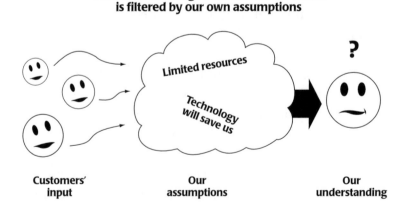

**Our understanding of the customers' needs
is filtered by our own assumptions**

Limited resources

Technology will save us

?

Customers'
input

Our
assumptions

Our
understanding

strategic plan, we must be critically self-aware of how we perceive the world and how those perceptions influence our thinking processes.

Challenge Assumptions by Applying the Five Whys

Most professionals are aware of the Japanese approach to root cause analysis—asking "Why?" five times to discover the root cause of a situation. If our thinking is the problem, we need to apply the five whys there as well. What do we think about a situation? Well, why is that so? And why do we think *that?* That's an interesting observation, why do we think *that?*

Asking ourselves "Why?" five times about our own thinking can make us more aware of our own assumptions and beliefs that affect our ability to listen to our customers and develop a strategic vision for quality. It is important for members of the planning team to be aware of their own assumptions. The quality manager needs to prod the team to question their assumptions if the team members are not doing this for themselves.

> Example: The governing council for a middle school embarked on a strategic planning session. Their first effort involved questioning their own assumptions about why the middle school existed. Early answers to this question suggested that the purpose of the school was to teach specific subjects. As the parents and teachers dug deeper and continued to ask "Why?" they came up with their deeper assumptions that the school existed to teach values and skills that would enable the students to become successful in high school and be oriented toward attending college.

Perceptions About Technology

One important aspect of our thinking about the world and our future involves how we understand the development and implementation of technology. It is helpful for people who are facilitating the strategic planning process to understand the manner in which knowledge about technology travels. The reason this is important to strategic planning is the tremendous link among technology, life, and organizations in our society. Many strategies for enhancing quality, such as process reengineering, rely on technological breakthroughs that can be harnessed in new ways to improve a process or system.

A useful model for understanding the migration of technology in the past was offered by the historian, Arnold Toynbee. Toynbee observed how a technological innovation, such as the minting of money, would be invented in one geographical location, and then, over time, the innovation would travel geographically to other areas. The use of coins spread gradually over the centuries from the Middle East to the Roman world, and from there coins were introduced to new people through trade and conquest. European explorers took the concept of coins with them as they traveled over land to the East and over water to the West. Toynbee called this process cultural radiation to describe the manner in which an innovative idea or technology extends outward from its point of origin.

Over time, the rate of development of innovations has increased dramatically. What used to be the radiation of a few ideas over centuries became the spread of many ideas over decades, and then hundreds of ideas within a year. Now there are thousands of ideas radiating around the planet within weeks and days.

Toynbee's idea of cultural radiation can be better understood in the contemporary global exchange of information and technology by the observations of John Naisbitt.

In his work, *Megatrends*,[1] Naisbitt observed that the spread of technology tends to follow the line of least resistance, meaning that it will first be used to improve previous technologies, and then will inspire new uses based on the technology itself. As Naisbitt noted, technological innovation does not travel in a straight line, but "weaves and bobs and lurches and sputters." Because your organization is harnessed to technology, you need to watch the weaving and lurching changes in technology that will revolutionize your opportunities in the future.

To find ways to understand the customers' needs, and seek new technological breakthroughs and applications that can meet those needs, you must listen in order to identify opportunities for change. Such an application is described in the following section.

Listening for the Opportunity

The key to listening to customers is to listen for the opportunities inherent in their needs. Opportunities basically come in two forms. Some utilize an existing technology or knowledge by matching it up with the customers' needs. Other opportunities provide no ready answer but might become a place to apply a new discovery once it is made.

For instance, in order to produce videocassette recorders, manufacturers needed to produce machined parts polished to mirror perfection. This machining technology existed as a result of its development for the nuclear weapons program. Someone recognized the opportunity to fill a need with an existing piece of knowledge (see Figure 2.3).

There are other opportunities waiting to be aided by new discoveries. For example, medical science needs new tools to combat many diseases that are based on problems

---

1. John Naisbitt, *Megatrends* (New York: Warner Books, 1982), 37.

Figure 2.3.   Listen for the Opportunities Inherent in the Customer's Needs

Types of opportunities	Examples
Use existing knowledge to meet a customer's need.	Combine the need to produce polished metal with a new machining technology.
Create new knowledge to meet a customer's need.	Create or discover strong ceramics for lighter automobile engines.

in genetic codes. Humanity stands on the threshold of the elimination of numerous genetic diseases through the knowledge that will be obtained from international studies of human DNA.

Often, the need for new knowledge and the unforeseen use of knowledge are closely connected. For instance, there is a need to lighten the weight of automobiles in order to increase fuel efficiency and, in the long run, avoid an oil crisis. Many researchers are working on an engine made from ceramics, which will weigh only a fraction of what a metal engine weighs. The first manufacturer to hit the market with a ceramic engine will have a major competitive advantage in selling fuel-efficient vehicles. On the other hand, the ceramic engine may be a breakthrough in another area that is currently stymied: the flying automobile. Prototype flying cars have been built using metal engines as fans to give cars the lift necessary to fly. Ceramic engines may provide the same lift and lower the vehicle's body weight. As you see, a breakthrough meant to solve one problem can create opportunities in other areas.

What does this have to do with strategic planning? If you want to achieve high quality in vacuum tubes or horse buggies, then go to it. Successful organizations, however, listen to their customers' needs, consider the technical possibilities, and put forth high-quality innovations that redefine their market. The possibilities of technical innovation (using it in its broadest term, including our social knowledge) create new levels of products and services and redefine the meaning of quality. The planning team is a vehicle for driving the process of listening to customers and identifying needs. The quality manager is the ideal person in the organization to champion this process.

Creating the Listening Moment

Since the first step in strategic planning is listening to the customer, it will help the planning team to reflect on the actions that can enhance our ability to listen. In describing the educational process, educators often speak of the "learning moment." It is a somewhat mystical point in time when an individual is ready to learn something. The background knowledge is there; the individual is focused on the situation; and the learning happens. The individual suddenly experiences an "ah-ha" moment when he or she puts things together to form a new understanding.

There is likewise a "listening moment" when people are somehow tuned in to hear something new and are ready to connect that new information with other knowledge to create an opportunity. It may or may not be possible to force the listening moment to occur, but it is certainly possible to create a setting that is conducive to listening and finding opportunities.

It is important for the planning team to create a listening moment when the customers' needs can be heard and understood. There are several proven methods for creating a climate conducive to listening, as shown in Figure 2.4. These methods include brainstorming, nominal group technique, focus group interviews, and the use of historical time lines, which are all well known in the quality field. While each tool has common uses, they all can also be used by the planning team to establish an opportunity to listen to the customers. All these methods share the common theme of gathering people together in a group to harness the collective ideas of the group, allowing their thoughts to sharpen as each person hears what the oth-

Figure 2.4. Tools That Can Help Create the Listening Moment

Tool	Application	Setting
Brainstorming	Create an image of what customers would like to achieve.	Group
Nominal group technique	Identify key issues to be addressed in a strategic plan.	Group
Focus groups	Encourage customers' critique of services.	Group
Time lines	Build a collective view of the past to help create a consensus about the future.	Group
Ask for their plan	Fast way to get to the customer's bottom line (if they know what it is).	Individuals
Survey	Ask customers' preferences about possible actions.	Individuals

ers share. In addition, there are methods for gaining input from customers through the use of surveys.

Brainstorming

The purpose of brainstorming, as it relates to strategic planning, is to create a setting in which customers and/or stakeholders can dream and create a better image of what they would like to have in the way of services or products and to discover how customers and stakeholders value a product or service. A brainstorming session should be conducted in a friendly environment, such as a comfortable conference room where participants are relaxed. A facilitator should be present to welcome the participants and thank them for taking the time to provide their opinions. The facilitator should then review the steps in brainstorming with all of the participants so everyone will know what to expect. The facilitator is responsible for ensuring that the session sticks to the guidelines. In some cases it may be important to stress that the ideas generated on the list will not be linked back to any individual.

The planning team should consider the groups of customers and stakeholders whose views and opinions are needed. The team will then compile a list of people who can speak for the needed groups. In some cases, the team will want to randomly select people from a list of known customers. In other cases, the team may want to be sure to include a spokesperson from the organization's largest customers. Or, the team may want to invite people who have expressed concerns in the past about the organization's products and services. The specific identity of the brainstorming group participants will depend on what the planning team is trying to accomplish. Here are the steps that the planning team can take to use brainstorming in this manner.

1. Gather together a group of ten to twenty people whose opinions are valued as representative of the perspective of some part of the organization's customer base. This group may represent diverse segments of the customers, such as age, gender, or cultural groups. For example, a city government might bring together people of different ages and from different parts of town to get a comprehensive view of their customers' needs.
2. Discuss the ground rules for brainstorming with the group, such as:
   • No critiquing of ideas as they are being generated.
   • Maintain a semblance of order.
   • If one does not have an idea, just pass.
3. The facilitator poses a question for the group and collects ideas from the group members, writing them where everyone can see them.
4. The facilitator guides the process to ensure that the rules are followed.
5. After the brainstorming, the facilitator involves the participants in reviewing their ideas, looking for common

themes and repeated ideas. Everyone makes sure that they understand what has been recorded.

From the perspective of strategic planning, the question to be given to the group will vary greatly from one setting to the next. The person leading the brainstorming exercise needs to consult with the organization's leaders to make sure that the right type of question is being asked in order to receive the appropriate input from the group.

For example, a question like the following might be posed: "If you could make any changes regarding the services you receive, what would you change?" Other possible questions are:

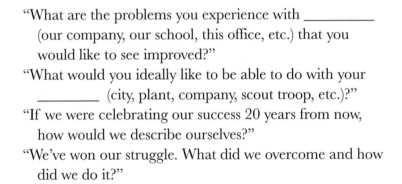

"What are the problems you experience with _____ (our company, our school, this office, etc.) that you would like to see improved?"

"What would you ideally like to be able to do with your _____ (city, plant, company, scout troop, etc.)?"

"If we were celebrating our success 20 years from now, how would we describe ourselves?"

"We've won our struggle. What did we overcome and how did we do it?"

Nominal Group Technique

Nominal group technique (NGT) is a method that builds on brainstorming to provide a process for people to evaluate the relative merit or importance of the ideas they have generated.

After the brainstorming process is complete and the ideas have been consolidated into single statements, each idea on the list is given a number. Participants are then asked to rank the best ideas in order of preference. If there is a long list, the participants might be asked to identify the seven best ideas. If it is a short list, they might be asked to identify the three best.

Nominal group technique provides a rapid method for finding a consensus on the key issues that need to be addressed in a strategic plan. When these meetings are conducted properly, the manager, school principal, or mayor's opinion does not outweigh other opinions by virtue of positional power. It is important to narrow the issues and ideas down to what Juran would call the "vital few." The strategic planning process needs to focus on the key issues that will most greatly impact the organization.

Another option for conducting the process is to take a list of brainstormed ideas and place them on large easel pages around the room. Give every participant a certain number of colored adhesive dots. Then ask each person to review the list of ideas and to place one dot by each of the ideas they consider to be most important. This method has the advantage of allowing people to quickly see which ideas received the most votes. This visibility can also be a drawback, since it may influence where people stick their final dots, since they will be able to see which ideas have received many dots and which have received few. One group at a manufacturing facility used this type of NGT, giving everyone a certain number of dots to place by the ideas they thought would best help the company solve its quality problems. The top manager in the meeting had trouble following the rules. He wanted to place all of his dots next to the one idea he thought was best. The process does require some facilitation.

Nominal group technique can also be employed to develop a two-dimensional image of opportunities for an organization. This can be done by first using NGT to identify what the important issues may be and then asking participants to

Figure 2.5. Comparing Importance and Effectiveness

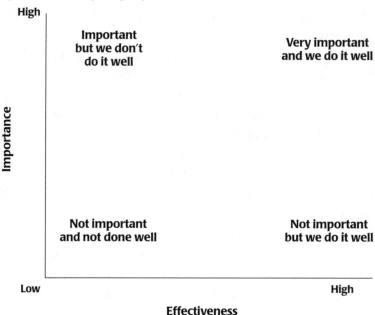

rank the items on their list as to how well the organization performs them. By comparing the ranking of importance to the ranking of effectiveness, participants can readily see where the organization does well in important tasks, and where it may perform poorly (see Figure 2.5). This exercise will also illustrate how well or poorly the organization is performing in unimportant areas.

For example, a city library system can use this idea to define which services are more important and how well they are being provided. A manufacturer can ask customers to rank the importance and effectiveness of specific product features.

Focus Groups

The focus group process can be employed in several different ways to support strategic planning. To aid in listening to the customers' needs and expectations, the focus group should consist of a representative sample of the organization's clients. These people are gathered together for a meeting, which may last an hour or two. A facilitator has a prepared list of questions to ask the focus group members. The questions can be open-ended or very specific. For example, a focus group for a school might include parents, students, and teachers. They might be asked open-ended questions regarding the direction they would like to see the institution pursue. They might also be asked specific questions regarding the quality of the library or the availability of financial support for students.

One organization that is involved in environmental restoration uses focus groups that consist of the residents in the vicinity of the site undergoing environmental cleanup. The organization will gather together people who represent the various geographic and economic interests around the cleanup site and ask specific questions to help determine what the residents think about the cleanup activities and what issues need to be addressed. The focus group's input gives the people conducting the cleanup very useful feedback about areas of concern and the residents' perceptions of the quality of work being performed by the environmental restoration organization. By listening to these customers (who are indirectly paying for this work as taxpayers), the organization was able to identify concerns about the process of educating people about the cleanup activities.

The key to effective use of the focus group methodology is good preparation. Make sure the group represents the stakeholders or customers you want to hear from. Have a well-prepared list of questions that will give you the information you want. This will enable your organization to prepare its own strategic plan and see which quality issues are of vital importance.

Time Lines

Another tool for helping people envision where to go with their future involves some exploration of where they have been in the past.

The team may want to work with a customer or client group to help develop a consensus regarding what future they collectively want to create. For instance, when planning for city government, it would be helpful to gather a group of stakeholders together. The doctors who refer their patients to a particular hospital might be brought together to find out what they desire in the future from the hospital. Business and community leaders might be brought together by a college or university to help determine the educational services needed by the community.

It is often useful to involve the group in creating a time line on a series of easel pads around a conference room. The first chart might identify issues, trends, or important events or people who influenced the organization twenty years ago. The second chart might cover the events and people that influenced the organization ten to fifteen years ago. A third chart would have information about events, trends, and people from five to ten years ago. A fourth chart would collect information that deals with the most recent years.

There are several important reasons for using a time line prior to looking at the future. First, the exercise builds a sense of perspective. It will provide a measure of realism regarding how the organization has changed, or failed to change. It will also create a common point of reference for everyone involved in the process.

Most people tend to lose track of where their organization has been over the last twenty years, if it has even existed that long. Remembering where we have been in the past helps us gain perspective regarding how far we have come, or how little may have actually changed. Either way, it is useful for people to tap in to this perspective as they start to brainstorm or dream about the future.

Figure 2.6. Example of a Time Line Used in a Planning Session With a City Government

1950s	1960s	1970s	1980s	1990s
Growth in housing due to new factories.	Federal funding to support housing inspection.	Loss of inspection funds.	Gradual increase in slum housing.	Major quality problem with housing.

For example, a time line exercise was used with a city government group that had been given the responsibility of developing a strategic plan to improve the quality of life in a downtown community (see Figure 2.6). The group consisted of people who were long-time residents of the community, and included professionals from city and county government, the police and fire departments, the school systems, and local businesses. This group was very diverse, not only in their economic situations and daily experience of life in the city, but also regarding their knowledge about how the city had evolved over the last thirty years. The time line exercise gave everyone an opportunity to share information regarding where the city had been. Long-time residents enjoyed the opportunity to share their knowledge with the newer professionals. The new professionals learned a great deal about how conditions had evolved into their current state. This exercise set the stage for identifying the major problems that the planning session would address.

Another group, in a business setting, used this same exercise to accomplish exactly the same effect. Those who were long-time members of the organization had the opportunity to share the history of the business that newer people did not know. The new people were afforded an opportunity to learn how the organization had evolved. The result was a more level playing field, in which the new people had more respect for the organization's veterans, and the old-timers had a chance to reflect on how the organization had changed. Everyone was well positioned to see which areas demanded change.

A time line provides a degree of realism regarding change. People can see that change sometimes comes slowly and sometimes occurs in great leaps. The outside forces and internal forces that create or resist change can be appreciated when we look at our organization's past.

Not everyone who participates in this exercise will have been around for twenty years. A time line allows newer people to learn important stories about the organization that usually do not come out in other ways. The exercise helps everyone form a similar perspective as to how the organization came to be the way that it is today. This sometimes creates a bond among the participants and helps them better understand other people's views about where the organization needs to go in the future.

Figure 2.7. Steps in Conducting a Time Line Exercise

1. Gather all the participants into one room.
2. Place easel pages on the room's walls, each designating a decade.
3. Starting with the earliest era, ask the participants to identify what significant things happened, who was in charge, what it felt like to be in the organization.
4. Continue on to the present, collecting ideas on the easel pages.
5. Ask people to summarize the major themes they see from this information.

The facilitator should ask the participants to look at the completed time line and identify major themes or trends that emerge from the drawing. As participants summarize the major themes they perceive from the time line, the facilitator should list these themes on an easel for everyone to see. These themes will be conditions that must be addressed in order to achieve a new vision.

Ask the Customer for Their Strategic Plan

Another approach for learning the customer's view of the future, when there is a single primary customer, is for the planning team to ask for a copy of their strategic plan, or to sit down with a manager from the customer's organization and find out what about the future is important to their organization.

Planning team members at an electrical power plant took this approach with the factories in their area. They asked each plant manager what the future needs of their organization would be and what concerns they had. The planning team learned that some plants were competing with factories in other regions that could buy their electricity at lower rates, giving them a competitive advantage in pricing their products. The planning team went back to their facility and began an aggressive campaign to cut costs in order to help their customers and maintain their client base. The central focus of the cost-cutting campaign was to look for waste and counter it by launching a quality improvement initiative.

As a result of their quality improvement effort, waste was reduced, operating efficiency improved due to enhanced maintenance, and other operating costs were reduced. This led to a lower cost for the customer that ensured that the customer continued to buy electricity from the plant, instead of buying it from another nearby power company. This also ensured that the customer could stay in business, providing long-term stability in sales for the utility company. The utility's managers took the time to learn what was important to their customers about the future, and shaped their strategy around the customers' needs.

Surveys

Surveys can also be used as a method for gathering customer information. Most surveys tend to be designed to gather feedback from customers regarding how they like or dislike a particular service. However, surveys can also be used to determine customers' preferences regarding possible actions an organization might initiate to meet their needs. A bank, for example, might survey customers regarding changes in their operating hours. A school's planning team can survey parents about ancillary programs that would help meet the changing demands created by blended families and dual-income families. A record company in Minnesota has a very specific list of people who like their music. This company sends out surveys to these customers, asking them what the company should produce next.

It is often a good idea to follow up a general survey with focus groups to better understand how customers feel about specific issues. Eye-to-eye contact with people in a focus group setting helps establish a clearer understanding of people's interest in and commitment to various ideas.

The data from surveys and the focus group feedback will help to identify issues and options to incorporate into the strategic plan. Ongoing surveys help in the revision and updating of the plan after it is established.

Ready, Aim, Fire

In the 1980s many companies tried to speed up their planning processes to quickly adapt to changing conditions. If anything was true from that decade that will be even more important in the new millennium, it is this need for organizations to be able to move quickly in defining their mission and vision.

However, in our zeal to be fast, we must not abandon the virtue of accuracy. Some organizations adopt a "Ready, fire, aim" philosophy to quickly plan and implement change. However, this is a formula for disaster for organizations that try it. No matter how fast you are on the draw, it does you no good if you miss the target. The right sequence is always "Ready, aim, fire." You just have to learn how to aim *fast*. So, while you take the time to listen to your customers, do not think the effort has to extend over many months. Most of the tools discussed in this chapter can be used in a matter of days to give you a good sense of the customers' needs.

The next chapters will help you aim fast to determine your organization's mission and vision and define the actions that are needed to move your organization in the right direction.

Baldrige and ISO 9000 Notes

It should be noted that "customer requirements and expectations and their expected changes" are the first items that the Baldrige criteria encourage organizations to seek in strategy development. Customer requirements in the Baldrige perspective extend to the price customers expect to pay, in addition to issues of reliability and performance. Listening to the voice of the customer must include hearing what the customer can afford to pay for a product or service.

ISO 9000 covers the issue of customer input to planning by noting that each organization has customers as stakeholders and that the stakeholders' "expectations and needs" must be addressed. The quality policy of each organization "shall be relevant to the supplier's organizational goals and the expectations and needs of its customers."

The Journey of Ten Thousand Miles

There is a well-worn Chinese proverb regarding the journey of ten thousand miles that begins with one step. It certainly applies as well to strategic planning. The first step in strategic planning begins with recognizing the need to listen to your customers. This realization leads to the selection of a method for creating a listening moment. The planning team may either get involved in dialogue with a key customer, choose a group process for identifying issues and opportunities, or opt instead for using statistically based surveys. In any of these cases, the goal is to find a way to listen to the customer. Once the team understands what the customers want, it is in a position to consider how the organization can work to meet these needs. Throughout this process, the quality manager must encourage the team to listen and support its taking the time to explore and develop a sound grasp of the information. This is essential for developing a strategic plan.

Chapter 3

Positioning to Meet the Customer's Needs

A Fortune 500 company sells a portion of its business to a former competitor. The company has studied its customers and its areas of greatest strength. A new emphasis is being placed on the strongest areas, which are closest to the company's core customers. Side ventures that were created to diversify the company and that do not support the company's primary customers are being sold.

A regional vocational school used to offer day and evening classes. The two classes appealed to two distinct groups of clients in the community. Day classes attracted young people right out of high school. Evening classes served adults who wanted to enhance their skills or pick up an extra skill. After listening to the students, studying the community's needs, and looking at their budget, the school administrators decided to cut back on the evening school program in order to put more resources into serving their primary clients, the daytime students.

An agricultural extension office within state government had clients who were heavily dependent on growing a single crop. The value of that cash crop had been declining over several years. To prepare for the future needs of the farmers, the agricultural agents began contacting state universities in the region to collect information on other options the farmers might be able to consider.

A local restaurant had been serving breakfast to their customers for several years. The popularity of breakfasts had been growing, but the preparation of individual dishes was labor intensive. In order to better serve their customers, the restaurant owner decided to put in a breakfast buffet. The number of customers went up and stayed up, while costs were held down.

These examples illustrate the need for organizations to position themselves to meet the needs of their customers. After listening to what the customers hope for, need, or even fear about the future, the strategic planning team must examine the organization to discover how it can best prepare to serve its customers. Sometimes this preparation means adding new products and services, or expanding on existing ones. Sometimes it means eliminating activities that do not really support the customer's needs. It is vital for the team to help the organization focus on its strongest areas and how it can establish world-class performance. If the organization allows its attention to be diluted, it will become or stay a mediocre Jack-of-all-trades.

Moving the organization into the best position to meet its customers' needs requires a considerable amount of thinking about the mission of the organization. In most cases, this process leads to the creation of a mission statement that will guide the organization's efforts to delight its customers and clients. In some cases a mission statement already exists, but the strategic planning team may find that the current mission statement misses the mark and needs to be revised.

Figure 3.1.   Planning to Meet the Customer's Needs

1. Prepare a mission statement.
2. Identify gaps between customer expectations and real practice.
3. Communicate the mission statement companywide.
4. Start making decisions based on the mission statement.

Understanding the Organization's Mission

Whether an organization serves the private, public, or volunteer sector, most people are familiar with the need for a mission statement. How effective an organization will be depends on how well the mission meets the needs of customers or clients, and on how well people in the organization understand the mission.

Some people will suggest that the mission of a business enterprise is to make money for the stockholders who invest in the business. Within that broad conception, anything goes. This philosophy can ruin a successful organization by defusing focus and energy from the central mission and wasting energy on side ventures about which the people in the organization have little expertise or passion. There are many examples, such as Sears, which diversified into the insurance field and many other endeavors some years ago. They lost their historical focus on retailing and were leapfrogged by new companies like Wal-Mart that kept their customers' needs in clear focus.

Effective organizations will develop a mission statement that embodies their purpose, focuses on meeting the needs of customers, and embraces quality as a core factor.

A mission statement is a public declaration for all of the organization's customers and stakeholders that gives direction as to what the organization exists to do. It guides how the organization will position itself to meet customers' needs. As a public statement, it should be concise and easily understood.

Figure 3.2.   Creating a Mission Statement

What	Why	How
A concise statement that expresses the core purpose of the organization.	Provides a focus for the organization. Serves as a guiding principle for the strategic plan.	Charter a team that represents all levels and perspectives within the organization.

Here are examples of mission statements for several types of organizations that illustrate how they can be used in government and business. A strategic plan can then be developed from the foundation established by the mission statement.

Drury Inn Mission Statement

Our mission is to provide excellent service and value to our guests through the successful and consistent operation of a growing system of quality overnight lodging facilities.

Saint Paul's Mission Statement

The City of Saint Paul is dedicated to providing its citizens with high-quality, responsive services which protect their safety and health, and enhance their quality of life. In striving for the most efficient, responsive, and cost-effective results, the city may directly provide these services, join in partnership with others, or act as a catalyst to ensure that services are provided.

Wolf's Restaurant Mission Statement

Our mission as a community-oriented specialty restaurant is to provide efficient, friendly, and courteous service while offering the highest-quality food products available to our patrons.

All of these examples focus on the customer as the driving force for the organization. In the City of Saint Paul's mission statement, the citizens are the customers and quality is clearly highlighted as a core value. The Wolf's restaurant mission statement also focuses on quality, with an emphasis on the customers' need for service. The mission statement from the Drury Inn, a fast-growing hotel company, likewise places a great emphasis on providing excellent quality services. It does not matter if the organization is as large as a city or as small as a family-owned restaurant, or a private business that operates across the nation; the mission statement that focuses on quality sets the right tone.

One of the most significant question about the mission statement is *who* should write it. Many organizations fall short in writing their mission statement by not involving their stakeholders in the creative process. If a single person, such as the top manager, sits down and writes a mission statement for the organization, it may or may not be dynamic and inspirational. Who will support it?

Opening the writing process up to the other managers is a step in the right direction. A group will have a better perspective than one individual. However, even as a group, there may be problems with writing a mission statement that will make sense later, out in the offices, shops, laboratories, and loading docks of the organization.

A more effective process for creating the mission statement is to recruit a diagonal slice of the organization as a team to write the statement. This could be the strategic planning team, or it could be a special team chartered just for this purpose. The quality manager should give the team some guidelines and establish the expectation that the mission statement will tell what the organization exists to do and that it will state the organization's emphasis on quality in accomplishing its mission. The diagonal slice should include senior and middle managers, front-line leadership, and individual contributors. Try to bring together the people who are highly enthusiastic. If the organization includes people who are represented by a bargaining unit, then invite its leadership to help in the creative process. Schools might include alumni as stakeholders and get them involved.

A mission statement that is created with input from all levels has a greater likelihood of being understood. Furthermore, when people throughout the organization learn that their peers helped create the mission statement, there is a greater likelihood that it will be accepted and is not just some form of propaganda. A truism of organizations is: "Those who create tend to support." People care more for a mission statement when they or their peers have been engaged in creating it.

Give the group drafting the mission statement a time limit. Ask to have it done within ninety minutes and you will probably get a product that meets your needs. Do not let the group labor for days on this and do not let them get bogged down over wordsmithing.

Figure 3.3.   Guidelines for Effective Mission Statements

1. State what the organization does:
   -Build houses   -Provide food services
   -Make widgets   -Repair roads
   -Teach children   -Rehabilitate drug users
2. State how quality relates to this purpose.
3. Define the relationship to the customers.

"What Should We Do?"

If you are answering the telephone for a business or government office that has a mission statement, you know what you are supposed to be doing. When the mission statement embraces quality as a fundamental principle of the organization, your actions—how you do your job every day—take on a new meaning. You are not just there to answer the phone, you are there to answer the phone in a way that helps make your office a world-class organization. The stated emphasis on quality provides a cue as to how you are to act, and why it is important.

This provides everyone in the organization with a standard they understand. Their purpose is not just to do a task, but to do that work in a manner that makes it the best it can possibly be. Including quality in the mission statement is the first real step toward building spirit and commitment in an organization. In effect, it is saying: "We, the people of this organization, have a mission which calls us to be the very best we can be, in our lives and with each other, as we seek to meet the needs of our customers."

The quality emphasis in the mission statement also serves to drive all the subsequent decision making in the organization. When the organization publicly proclaims that quality is an essential factor in success, then it becomes a factor that people consider as they make both major policy decisions and minor day-to-day decisions. The emphasis legitimizes the focus on customers' needs and empowers people to speak out about actions that are inconsistent with the philosophy.

Every day, in any organization, there are large and small choices to make. What are the accepted criteria in the organization for making these choices? Is it the lowest cost? Is it the fastest turnaround? Or, is it the best quality for the customer?

Recognizing the Gaps Between Theory and Practice

Usually there is a gap between where the organization wants to be and where it is right now regarding its mission statement. The gaps must be recognized and addressed in order to avoid creating a situation where people perceive the organization is saying one thing but doing something else. A school may talk about quality education but not make investments to upgrade the library. A state agency may talk about serving the citizens but only stay open during daytime hours when most citizens are working. A company may talk about producing quality products but neglect to control incoming raw materials.

Donald Schon, a social scientist, has written about the gap that often exists in organizations between the "espoused theory" and the "theory in use." Schon observed that organizations often say one thing and actually do something else. Therefore, if an organization espouses quality, but takes actions that are not consistent with achieving quality, there will be some tension within the organization. This tension is very valuable to the organization, because it is this tension that creates the changes that are needed for organizations to renew themselves and survive.

For example, consider a small plastics manufacturer seeking to improve the quality of its products in order to keep its business as a supplier to a major automotive manufacturer. The lack of improvement activities on the shop floor inspite of the "quality talk" soon created a crisis. People heard one thing and saw another, and they became angry. They knew their jobs were at risk if quality standards were not achieved, so employees and managers alike began to point out the gaps. This crisis was positive because it propelled people to take action toward improving quality, including the implementation of training and teams to utilize statistical tools. In this case, the tension between espoused theory and theory in use was a dynamic source for change.

If an organization does not claim to uphold quality, then there will be no tension when quality is not valued on a daily basis. People will accept the notion that it is okay not to meet the customer's needs, whether that is an external customer or the person down the hall in the next workstation. Without an emphasis on quality in the mission statement, there is no standard with which people can compare their actions and identify their deficiencies. Its absence is a green light to everyone in the organization to look the other way when there are problems concerning quality.

Even when an organization is far from meeting its goal it is better to *have* the goal toward which people can strive. When the mission statement has been created by a cross-section of stakeholders, there will be greater willingness in the organization for people to speak up when they encounter the gap.

A mission statement should encourage people to evaluate their decisions and actions based on the impact they have on the quality objective. Are we hiring the most qualified people who can produce the best results? Are we procuring the appropriate materials to achieve our goals? How do our customers perceive the quality of our services and products?

On one level, strategic planning is a process that defines the broad objectives in an organization. On another level, the merger of strategy and quality encourages the right types of day-to-day questioning and decision making that lead to more profitable and worthwhile organization.

Communicating the Mission

Having a mission statement that embraces quality is not much use unless the statement is communicated to everyone in the organization. The organization's mission statement should be used in new employee orientation, in the organization's newsletter, posted in the workplace, cited in meetings, and spoken of in conference rooms.

When an organization goes to a lot of effort to develop a new mission statement, there should be an equal amount of effort to get the word out to the employees and customers, alike. This is the best way to reorient people's thinking about their role in helping the organization achieve its goal. They should discuss the mission statement and feel encouraged to point out areas where current practices do not live up to its message. These problem areas must be addressed for the organization to be successful. If the organization preaches quality, but uses poor raw materials, the employees will see the inconsistency, so empower them to point out the inconsistencies.

Failure to acknowledge these problem areas will undermine the positive effect of having a mission statement and will create cynicism among the employees. Consider how automobile manufacturers give production line workers a rope they can pull to stop the production line when there is a problem. It is wholly consistent with their espoused theory of quality. What kind of "rope" do people in your organization have to reach for when they see an action that is inconsistent with your quality ethic?

The mission statement should be a key component in any quality-related training conducted within the organization. It provides relevance to the training by linking it to the fundamental reason for being within the organization. Internal awards and recognition programs should likewise be linked to the mission statement so that people understand the context in which their actions are being rewarded.

Orienting New Employees to Quality

Many organizations underinvest in orientation for their new employees. The mission statement should be the starting point. It should also be used in publications that go out to all the stakeholders who are not internal to the organization. For example, a school's mission statement should be part of its recruitment literature so that parents and potential students understand what the school is about. A publisher's mission statement helps potential writers know what market niche the publisher serves. A volunteer agency's mission statement helps potential volunteers and contributors know what activities they will be supporting.

The synergy of combining the traditional strategic planning function with the quality emphasis opens up a powerful way to orient employees and to align them with the organization's mission.

Mission Statements Within the Organization

In addition to the organization's overall mission statement, subgroups in large organizations need to have separate mission statements that are also created in a participative manner. The maintenance organization in a factory can create its own statement to help define its important role in supporting the factory's mission. The library at a university can create a mission statement to support the mission of the university. The water treatment department in a city can develop its own mission statement to support the mission of the city government.

As with the larger organization's mission statement, the subgroup mission statement needs to address its purpose, its relationship to customers, and its focus on quality, along with other specifics that might be appropriate.

A team at the Safety and Health Division at a large Lockheed Martin manufacturing plant developed the following mission statement to help their co-workers understand how they supported the production mission of the facility.

Safety and Health Division Mission Statement

The mission of the Safety and Health Division is to provide program leadership in order to achieve an unsurpassed safety and health culture. We will do this by empowering our people, fostering teamwork, and being agents of change so as to provide services of long-term value and to achieve cost-effective compliance with regulations.

Note how this example focuses on quality without using the word itself? "An unsurpassed safety and health culture" and "services of long-term value" communicate their focus on quality. Specific steps to achieve this are highlighted, such as "empowering our people," "fostering teamwork," and "being agents of change."

With this statement, people can figure out what they should be doing and can appropriately challenge behaviors that contradict it.

Developing local mission statements that support the larger statement provides the opportunity for people to work with the overall organization's mission and to discover how their part of the organization should best contribute. Many groups within organizations tend to focus inwardly, often feeling like victims because other groups receive more funding or newer offices or larger budgets. Focusing the local group on how to support the mission of the overall organization helps people at the local level see why their role is important and gives them a perspective as to why other parts of the organization are important as well.

As with the formulation of the organization's broad mission statement, subgroups' mission statements should be created through a participative process as well. The maintenance organization within a factory, campus, hospital, or office building can have a mission statement that defines what maintenance there is to do and how this mission supports the larger organization. A diagonal slice of people in the maintenance group will increase the likelihood of producing a mission statement that is understood and accepted by everyone in the maintenance organization. The principle holds true for every other part of the larger organization.

To create these subgroup mission statements, the team must start by looking at the overall mission statement and think of the service they provide to the whole organization, and then align their statement to the needs of their internal customers. Failure to do so will lead to introverted, self-serving goals that sub-optimize the organization's resources and create conflict instead of community.

Being participative does not mean being slow. A team can be tasked to develop a supportive mission statement quickly. Set a boundary of one hour and challenge the team to work within that time frame.

Figure 3.4.   Benefits of a Mission Statement With a Strong Quality Emphasis

- Guides macro-level decisions about areas to emphasize.
- Encourages employees to speak out about inconsistencies that will damage the organization.
- Builds quality into the roots of the organization.

Making Tough Decisions

The mission statement, with its emphasis on quality, provides the criterion by which important choices are going to be made. It becomes the guiding factor in positioning the organization to best use its resources and to divert resources from areas that do not really address the organization's core needs.

Hospitals, for instance, are having to re-think their mission statements in many communities. Earlier mission statements led to hospitals becoming centers for walk-in patients who did not have a family doctor. This type of healthcare is not what most hospitals really need to provide. In the college system, the mission statement provides the boundaries regarding which academic disciplines will be taught and which will not. While there may be a need for technical training in a community, a liberal arts college would not step outside of its mission in order to offer classes on precision machining for a new factory. A publishing company focuses its mission on meeting the needs of a specific market segment. Their mission statement causes them to turn down offers to publish books that do not relate to their market.

Poorly written mission statements attempt to leave the door open for all options. "We are here to provide high-quality work for whatever anybody wants us to do" is a common trap, especially in organizations that rely on public funding.

A clear mission statement defines the area where the organization will focus energy to meet a customer's need. When energy and resources are being used in a manner that does not meet these needs, then some tough decisions have to be made.

On the broader level, a company, school, or agency must determine which of its activities do not support the mission. This may be a slow or fast process, but either way, there will be people who have an emotional attachment to work that is being performed who will not want to see it go away. The organization's leadership bears the responsibility for this assessment. The leader may consult with stakeholders or survey its customers, but the final responsibility for checking the organization's actions against the mission statement resides with the formal leadership, be it a chief executive officer, dean, president, principal, or director.

In the regional vocational school example at the beginning of this chapter, some teachers preferred to teach evening classes. Some also preferred to work with older adults instead of recent high school graduates. However, when the mission of the facility was examined, and when the resources were assessed to determine how to best accomplish the mission, it was apparent that the evening courses did not support the mission and detracted resources from it as well. Surely some people were unhappy with the decision; some may have left because of it, while others may have mourned the loss of the evening classes. However, everyone could understand the rationale for the decision, and most could see that the change would strengthen the quality of the programs being offered for the core clients of the institution.

Leadership's role is to ensure a fair and informed evaluation of activities and to align them with the organization's mission. Failure to perform this task will result in wasted resources and loss of focus. This process is akin to pruning a rose bush or fruit tree to stimulate healthy growth.

The mission statement, with its emphasis on quality, is not only useful in making decisions on the higher level, but also serves to guide decision making on the day-to-day level. Supervisors and employees have evidence that a commitment to quality and improvement is a core part of their jobs. Many individual office areas, shops, labs, and factory lines can utilize the mission statement as a guiding principle for determining how work should be conducted.

With an emphasis on quality in the mission statement, quality becomes a legitimate topic for discussion in the workplace. Some readers may be surprised to find that this is not always the case. To point out a problem means to point out that everything is not perfect. Some supervisors and mid-level managers cannot accept this from people below them in the organization. They consider it criticism and may even punish employees who seek to make improvements. This is the reason that Deming included "drive out fear" among his famous 14 points (see Chapter 4).

A mission statement that upholds quality is important to encourage continuous improvement in the organization. With this emphasis, people in the organization are encouraged to determine whether or not steps in a process really add value. The need to analyze processes and examine systems can become a legitimate role for supervisors and all employees in an organization, at every level.

Problems with Fuzzy and Conflicting Missions

Some organizations exist as if two or more separate entities had been welded together. In an effort to keep overall financial balance as the economy changes, many organizations diversify, merging unrelated fields, such as commodities and high technology, or retail merchandising and investment banking. One part of the organization has a mission and set of customers in one area, while another part of the organization has a different mission with a whole different set of customers. This creates a problem for the strategic planning process. The customers may be too diverse to listen to clearly. The meaning of quality may be radically different in the different types of business.

Where this problem exists, the best approach is to create mission statements that focus on the needs of the customers in specific areas. A monolithic mission statement cannot possibly have any meaning in an organization that possesses a multiple personality.

This also applies to state governments, state university systems, and federal agencies. The needs of customers in one geographic region may be quite different from those in another region. Senior management can best achieve overall quality by allowing each region to develop its own mission statement and use that to drive the quest on a local level.

Baldrige and ISO 9000 Notes

Incorporating quality into the organization's mission statement will establish the importance of quality as the organization's "true north" for organizations that use the Baldrige assessment process as a quality compass.

For organizations that employ the ISO 9000 standard for guidance, the focus on quality in the mission statement provides support for the required quality management system.

Chapter 4

Creating a Vision and Values to Guide the Development of the Strategic Plan

The mayor of the city stood before a community group to ask for input regarding what local government needed to do to improve the town. The mayor had formed these ad hoc community groups in every neighborhood to ensure that the interests of all the citizens were being heard and addressed. Through actions such as this she demonstrated a strong personal commitment to all the people in the city, not just to the wealthy subdivisions on the edge of town.

The managers decided that they would make decisions about production based on data. In the past, when an employee made scrap on his machine, he had to stay over on his own time to make up for the lost production. However, with the use of statistical tools, the managers learned that the machine was not capable of making good product 100 percent of the time, in spite of the operator's efforts. Management decided to stop punishing people for making scrap and started to focus on improving the system.

The desk clerk gave the guest a card to fill out that asked the guest about the hotel's service. Suggestions and problems were then discussed with the appropriate hotel staff in order to continuously improve the operation of the facility. Everyone in the hotel understood that the guests were the people who paid their salaries, and that satisfying them was of paramount importance.

The manager was retiring after more than thirty years with the company. He had been closely involved in the early efforts to implement Deming's philosophy in the 1980s. Reflecting on Deming's 14 Points, the manager noted, "There's a lot of fear in this organization, but I'm afraid to talk about it."

Once an organization has a mission statement in place, the strategic planning team may feel ready to jump in and start developing a strategic plan. However, organizations often need to invest some time in reflecting on their vision and values, since these will strongly influence the content of the strategic plan. The quality manager will need to advise the planning team on whether or not to consider a vision or values statement prior to developing a plan. Existing vision statements may need to be reevaluated by the planning team to determine if they are still valid. The strategic plan provides the path that the organization will follow in order to achieve its mission and vision. The values statement guides the organization in choosing its path.

Figure 4.1.   Mission Statement and Vision

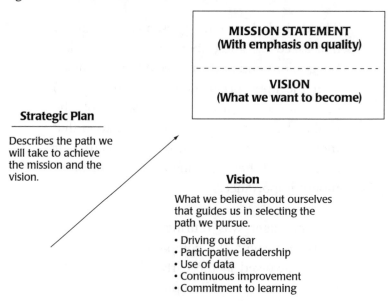

Strategic Plan

Describes the path we will take to achieve the mission and the vision.

MISSION STATEMENT
(With emphasis on quality)

- -

VISION
(What we want to become)

Vision

What we believe about ourselves that guides us in selecting the path we pursue.

• Driving out fear
• Participative leadership
• Use of data
• Continuous improvement
• Commitment to learning

Linking Mission and Vision

While the mission statement defines the purpose and direction of the organization, there must also be a vision, or a statement of values, which allows people inside the organization to know how to behave. It is both an internal and an external document; as a public statement of what the organization seeks to achieve, it also makes everyone inside the organization aware of the mission. But there are many ways in which people can work and behave so there is a need to define the boundaries in which people will work.

The mission statement defines the "what" about the organization, the organization's purpose. The "how" of the organization, how to act internally and with external groups, needs to be established in order for everyone to know what behavior will be acceptable. An internal vision statement, or set of values, defines the standards of behavior by which people are to conduct themselves.

Experienced facilitators will uniformly agree that people have an easier time achieving consensus about what actions should be taken when they first can agree about the principles upon which actions should be based. The time invested in defining a vision will be regained many times over when the time comes to select and implement the best actions.

Vision Statements

A vision statement builds on the mission statement by creating an image of what the organization must become in order to achieve the mission. For instance, a mission statement should define the purpose of the organization, such as: sell automobiles, make stoves, teach children. Each mission statement may involve the concept of quality—selling high-quality automobiles, producing world-class stoves, or providing excellence in education. But these statements do not offer any guidance about how to achieve those things.

Figure 4.2. Developing a Vision Statement

What	Why	How
A statement of what the organization is to become.	Gets people to agree in principle on what is important for the organization to do.	Strategic planning team discusses what they want the organization to become over time.

The vision statement will set a guide for how the selling of automobiles will be done. Perhaps the dealer envisions an organization where teamwork and cooperation are an everyday aspect of conducting business, where sales and maintenance staff will support each other. Perhaps the dealer wants to have a positive image in the community by supporting local charities. Or maybe the dealer wants to have a reputation of honesty and integrity in all sales and therefore restricts the amount of haggling in selling and trading cars.

Without the vision statement, the individuals in an organization are not grounded in any common set of beliefs and expectations. When the boundaries are not defined, people will act as they see fit, and their actions, while immediately beneficial to themselves, may be harmful to the entire group in the long run. For instance, if there is no value placed on cooperation within an organization, the default position is often for everyone to look out for their own best interests. In the automobile dealership example, this might mean that the salesperson will commit maintenance to have a new car ready for a customer before it is possible for maintenance to complete the work. The salesperson thinks, "That's not my problem. I did my job and made the sale, let them get busy and take care of the customer." The problem is, some other customer will be offended when their service is delayed in order for the maintenance department to take care of the mistake.

Like a mission statement, the vision should be prepared by a representative group of stakeholders. People in the organization need to help create the vision in order to enforce it. Once it is established, the vision statement should be posted for everyone to see. Behaviors that contradict the vision must be pointed out for resolution, especially if the inconsistent behavior comes from the top of the organization.

Here is an example of a vision statement from a city and county government strategic planning session conducted in Kentucky. The people who created this statement were a task force representing a diverse cross-section of the community.

Paducah and McCracken County Vision Statement

To empower the people of Paducah and McCracken County through the coordinated efforts of government, community groups, and residents to create a renewed community, which includes:

- Job opportunities for all citizens made available through training, education, entrepreneurial incentives, and capital resources.
- Safe and affordable housing for all citizens through new focus on neighborhood revitalization, development of sidewalks and street lights, and ownership opportunities.
- Recreational, educational, developmental, and job opportunities that recognize the specific needs and problems of youths.
- Expanded and coordinated volunteer programs to meet the evolving needs of the population.
- One-stop access to information and services.
- A crime-free, clean, culturally harmonious, and caring environment.

This vision statement was developed by a group of elected officials, administrative officers in city government, and community leaders. They conducted numerous focus group sessions with citizens and listened to many expressions of need and hope for their community. They adopted this final vision statement based on a draft prepared by their support staff.

This vision statement provides the city employees, citizens, and volunteer workers with a common reference point for the broad objectives of the city and county government. It outlines the key areas of concern within the community and will help people make decisions that support the vision.

How to Prepare a Vision Statement

One of the best ways to involve a group in preparing a vision statement is to ask them to imagine that it is ten years in the future. The organization has been highly successful in accomplishing its mission. The people in the room are gathered here to celebrate their success. Ask them to identify the attributes, factors, or conditions that have made them successful.

This exercise causes people to project their thoughts into the future, escaping the current realities. It taps into their personal vision—often unspoken until then—for what they want their organization to be.

It is usually best for a facilitator to collect people's ideas on an easel pad and then ask the group to identify the common themes and key points. The vision statement can be roughed out in about an hour. It is usually best to give the rough version to a single person for final wordsmithing, which is then fed back to the group for any adjustments. Do not try to have a large group spend time on polishing the rough version into a final version.

A Values Statement

Some organizations may find a vision statement a rather abstract concept, meaning it is not perceived as concrete enough to guide people's actions. In those situations, a straightforward statement of the organization's values will work just as well.

Figure 4.3.   Developing a Values Statement

What	Why	How
A formal statement of the values held to be important within the organization.	Gives people guidance on how to act in different situations.	Representative team discusses and agrees on values.
	Identifies common ground that people share.	

Gaining consensus on values prior to establishing the strategic plan offers significant advantages. When people can find common ground for their beliefs about what is acceptable and desirable behavior, then the actual planning process becomes easier. A values statement defines for everyone in the organization what the key values are. Like the vision statement, the values statement guides people on how to act in situations that require judgment, such as prioritizing customers' needs.

A values statement has a greater likelihood of being useful and accepted when it is created in a participative manner. For top management alone to define the values is to say to the rest of the organization that their thoughts do not count.

The following is an example of a values statement from an organization that is involved in manufacturing, research, and environmental restoration:

Lockheed Martin Energy Systems Values Statement

Concern for People
- Protect the health and safety of our employees and the environment around us.
- Treat each person with respect, fairness, openness, and trust.
- Strive to provide challenging, secure employment with opportunities for growth and creativity.
- Pay for performance and recognize excellence.

Working Together
- Achieve the participation and involvement of all employees.
- Encourage clear two-way communication at all levels.
- Promote teamwork with all employees and organizational units, the leadership of our unions, and our customers.

- Be good neighbors and participate in improving the quality of life of the communities around us.

Challenging Goals
- Be known as a high-quality organization in all that we do.
- Continue to improve our products, processes, and services.
- Accept change as an opportunity and provide conditions and policies that help us work effectively.
- Be responsible stewards of all the resources entrusted to us.
- Seek new opportunities of national importance.

This specific organization uses its values statement in all aspects of its management, and especially in setting strategy. The emphasis on being "known as a high-quality organization" influences the type of work that the company seeks and the internal standards of performance. The emphasis on continuous improvement lays the foundation for an active total quality management process. The organization's value regarding "participation and involvement of all employees" drives an internal emphasis on empowerment. The values statement influences strategic business decisions, human resource decisions, and community relations issues as well as setting the tone for the strategic planning process.

How to Prepare a Values Statement

The values statement can be prepared by the planning team or by a special group called together for this purpose. If a group is chartered to create a values statement, it should represent a diversity of opinions and perspectives in the organization. Diversity, in this case, could mean the perspectives of senior management, middle management, and front-line employees. Or, it could mean mixing the headquarters staff with representatives from different facilities of the same organization. Diversity also means balancing the participation of men and women, different racial groups, unions, or any other group whose voice needs to be heard.

Gather the appropriate people together and break into small groups to brainstorm issues and concerns. Then ask each group to share what they came up with and make a list of common issues. Organize those issues into logical categories, such as concern for people, challenging goals, or teamwork. Then, draft a statement of values that addresses each category.

This process can be accomplished within a couple of hours. It is often advantageous to assign one person from the group to prepare a "straw man" document for the group to use as a basis for a final critique. This approach worked well for the Continental Congress when they sent Thomas Jefferson and some advisors off to write a Declaration of Independence, and it can work for you.

The organization's values statement must be agreed to by the senior-level people, and afterwards shared with everyone in the organization. In some places, every employee is given a wallet card with the organization's mission statement, vision, and values printed on it.

What Values Impact Quality?

What types of values might be important? Certainly emphasis on trust, loyalty, mutual support, honesty, and commitment to the group would be good starting places. However, there are other worthwhile issues such as the decision to use participative leadership styles and systematic use of data in decision making. The implementation of a process for continuously improving performance is yet another value. When organizations attempt to make changes that are not anchored in core values, the changes often are simply dismissed as the program of the month.

Since the values define what the people in the organization believe and guide them in selecting the path they will pursue to achieve their mission, it is appropriate to explore five core values that are essential to the foundation for a successful strategic plan:

1. Driving out fear.
2. Participative leadership.
3. Use of data.
4. Continuous improvement.
5. Commitment to learning.

Driving Out Fear

When Deming spoke of the need to drive fear out of organizations, he was making an important statement about the values that any group must possess to effectively compete. Effective organizations create a work environment in which people feel safe and appreciated for speaking out constructively about problems.

If organizations want to produce with quality, they must encourage employee suggestions for improvement without fear of retribution. The first step on the road to continuous improvement is the recognition of problems and opportunities when they exist.

Simply making the claim that everyone in the organization is free to point out problems and opportunities does not make it so. To create the desired environment, managers must ensure that every work group conducts regular meetings to share business information and seek employees' ideas about opportunities for improving quality, reducing costs, reducing cycle times, and providing better responses to customers. The follow-up on these ideas is a major part of management's role in the organization.

When there is no commitment to drive out fear, the quality effort will only be a shallow program that fails to address the root causes of problems.

When organizations develop a strategic plan that is not based on the value of driving out fear, the plan becomes skewed toward over-inspection, over-control, and punishment of people who raise questions. This type of situation causes people to disguise the cause of problems, cover up the evidence, and spend their energy on assigning blame to other people.

Autocratic and Democratic Leadership

When an organization makes a commitment to achieve high quality, it requires the commitment and participation of the entire work force to make it happen. People cannot be ordered to participate; they can be invited and encouraged to help the organization become more effective. However, once people start to participate, they expect to be treated as partners in the decision-making process.

Organizations that are achieving high quality are doing so by combining the knowledge of the quality profession with the insights of the organizational development field. Together, the quality and organizational development experts create a climate where people can work within defined boundaries to have ownership over their work.

This new style of workplace demands that a high value be placed on democratic leadership. Autocratic leadership undermines the willingness of people in any work setting to contribute ideas; this type of leadership robs people of a sense of work ownership and reduces employees to a state of apathetic compliance with management's dictates.

The importance of creating a highly participative work environment has been emphasized by researchers who have studied the factors that contribute to successful organizations. In his review of the famous Hawthorne experiment test room, Elton Mayo observed that productivity increased as long as the participants were free from coercion and that the major concern for managers "must be that of organizing teamwork."[1] Rensis Likert summarized the findings of numerous research studies to show that whether you are looking at production workers, supervisors, or research scientists, higher productivity is achieved when people have freedom to participate in the decision making that affects their work.[2] The management literature of the last five years has exploded with case after case of enhanced quality and productivity when organizations choose to become more democratic in their decision making.

Not all decisions in an organization need to be made in a highly participative manner. Certain types of decisions are appropriate for a single person to make. However, since the quality of work processes often depends on interrelated and interdependent actions, decisions should be presumed to require collaboration until proven otherwise.

Being participative in no way means lowering standards of conduct and accountability. In fact, a participative organization places a greater burden—the burden of ownership—on all its members to enforce expectations.

Use of Data in Decision Making

To achieve high quality, managers and everyone in the workplace must place a high value on using data for making decisions. In the past, many managers led on the basis of hunches

---

1. Elton Mayo. *The Social Problems of an Industrial Civilization* (Andover, MA: Andover Press, 1945).
2. Resnis Likert. *New Patterns of Management* (New York: McGraw-Hill, 1961).

and instinct. On average, this is no better than flipping a coin. Decision making must be grounded in data that gives people a basis for making choices.

In the managerial ranks, a commitment to using data means an understanding of how statistical variation occurs within systems. It is necessary to be able to distinguish common cause from special cause variation before jumping to conclusions. Managers must be able to distinguish real trends in their data from the variation that is a natural part of their system.

In the workplace, a commitment to using data means having performance indicators for work and using statistical tools to assess information. Performance indicators should be posted in every work area. Without this feedback, people often think they are doing a wonderful job, when in fact, there may be room for considerable improvement. Basic statistical tools such as flow charts, run charts, Pareto charts, and control charts should be developed and utilized in every work area in order to give people the data they need to make sound decisions on an ongoing basis.

While Deming's 14 Obligations for Management cover a wide range of concepts, the primary emphasis of his points was the essential need for managers to make decisions based upon sound statistical data in order to achieve long-term success. Instead of using fear, quotas, goals, or slogans to motivate people, Deming argued that people need useful data to help them make decisions to move toward success.

Without a commitment to using data, people in the organization will believe it is the organization's norm to make decisions in irrational ways. Decisions will be based on "gut feel," anecdotal information, prejudice, and wishes. People will feel justified in ignoring data that does not support their expectations, leading to failures.

A few years ago, the personnel managers of a large production facility decided their plant had a problem with absenteeism. The source of the problem was obviously visible to this group of middle-aged white men. According to their personal observations, there were too many young women out for maternity leave. Someone suggested that they study the data to confirm this belief. Reluctant to waste time on this, the managers nevertheless ran the attendance data. To their surprise, the data indicated that the group of people with the highest rate of absenteeism was middle-aged men who were out with back problems. A little bit of data can make a big difference in how we perceive the world and can greatly change the path on which we proceed to accomplish our missions.

An Ethic of Continuous Improvement

Perhaps the most important value for any organization to claim is the commitment to continuous improvement. Inherent in this value is the willingness to support critical self-examination with the recognition that any system can be improved. Finding new ways to improve is not a condemnation of the past or present, but a statement that every individual and organization is a living entity that can better itself.

The value of continuous improvement must be carried out by every leader in the organization on a day-to-day basis. Every staff meeting must devote some time to seeking opportunities for improvement. New ideas should receive followup. People who take the lead in the continuous improvement of their part of the organization must be recognized and rewarded.

Organizations that seek to protect the status quo will eventually be overwhelmed by others that are able to seek out and master new ways of doing work. To deny the ethic of continuous improvement is to set one's goals on just getting by.

Juran provided a great deal of insight into the ethic of continuous improvement, pointing out that improvements do not simply happen in an organization because people are well-motivated. Improvements only happen when individuals or groups get organized to study processes and implement changes. This requires a commitment on management's part to encourage questions, provide time for analysis and data collection, and create a structure suitable for managing continuous improvement.

A Commitment to Learning

Many organizations have come to recognize the need for a commitment to lifelong learning as a primary value. An organization can only succeed when its members have the skills and knowledge necessary to accomplish their mission. In former years, a person could learn to perform a task, or master the core knowledge of a profession, and count on several decades of stability in their work, needing to make only occasional refinements to their knowledge. Today there is a knowledge revolution that escalates the volume and diversity of knowledge and skills needed in any workplace.

No one can enter the workplace with all the knowledge and skills needed to perform effectively on an ongoing basis. Therefore, organizations are providing ongoing educational and training opportunities to keep their employees current in knowledge and skills. Even if an organization could hire new people with exactly the right skill mix, those skills would need major enhancements within three years, just to stay current with technology.

Since the field of applied statistical knowledge has yet to enter the high school curriculum, it is very important for organizations to educate people regarding the proper use of statistical tools and data. Deming referred to this as the "sixth principle for transformation of American industry." The primary issue to address, according to Deming, was the development of an understanding of variation. Most organizations will be much more effective in their use of data and their decision making when this understanding of variation exists.

Baldrige and ISO 9000 Notes

In ISO 9000 language, the values statement may serve very well as the organization's quality policy.

In organizations following the Baldrige criteria, the vision statement describes where the organization wants to be in terms of "overall performance and competitive leadership." This is the core of the quality-centered strategic plan. Establishing the vision is the part of the process from which the specific "actionable key business drivers" will emerge. Without a vision an organization will have an empty process.

Chapter 5

Scanning the Future

> "If you don't know what business you are in,
> conceptualize what business it would be useful
> for you to think you are in."
>
> *John Naisbitt,* Megatrends

Chapter 1 introduced several broad steps that comprise the process for strategic planning for an organization and the role of the quality manager in carrying out this process.

Chapter 2 focused on the first step, in which the planning team tries to understand the needs of the customers. Chapter 3 investigated the process for planning how the organization will meet those needs. Chapter 4 examined the need to provide internal alignment within organizations so that everyone can contribute to the overall goals.

This chapter will consider concepts and actions that enable effective participation in the strategic planning process. This chapter will also address the observations of educators and futurists who have dealt with problems associated with the study and design of the future.

The success of the strategic planning process depends on the ability to think of the future as an environment that is shaped and formed through plans and actions. Since the future is what people make of it, organizations cannot passively wait for events to unfold but must take proactive steps to understand and influence it.

Several specific problems, such as reification, educated incapacity, and self-fulfilling prophecies will be examined. This chapter will also discuss a widely used process of scanning the future in order to chart a course and will examine the benefit of having a variety of options.

Figure 5.1 illustrates a process for scanning the future in order to develop the specific objectives in the strategic plan. Scanning the future allows people to consider several scenarios of the future and recognize the forces at work that will help or hinder them in achieving their mission.

Figure 5.1.   Scanning the Future

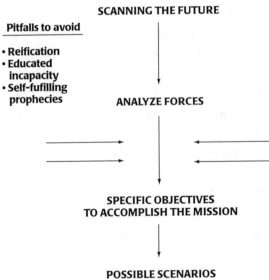

Reification

Reification is the belief that a system that has been created by people cannot be changed by people. Habitants of impoverished rural villages or urban slums learn to accept a line of reasoning that teaches them that they have no power to change the world around them, therefore, they are better off not trying to create change.

Reification, as a thinking process, is not confined to the Third World or just to the poor. Many communities and organizations have sat almost paralyzed as adverse change hit them, taking no action out of the false belief that action would be futile. Employees and managers have done nothing while factories closed, blinded by reification that led them to believe there was no point in struggling to keep the factory open.

As it relates to strategic planning, reification is one of the primary causes of failure in organizations. Reification stifles the planning process before it can even begin, by convincing people that there is no point in planning since things simply cannot be changed. For a strategic planning process to succeed, there must be sufficient belief within the organization that the future can be changed and that the people in the organization can influence its future.

Figure 5.2.   Reification

The signs:

"Other companies (schools, agencies, cities, hospitals, etc.) may be able to do those things (quality revolution), but it can't happen here."

"That's fine for the automotive industry, but it doesn't relate to us."

"They could do it because their conditions were just right. Things are different here."

The cure:

• Training
• Benchmarking
• Conferences
• Information campaigns

The quality manager and the planning team can combat reification by using other organizations as examples of proactive thinking and action. In manufacturing, the quality manager should use examples of other companies that made a turnaround. Xerox is a great example for general use, but try to find an example in your specific industry. People who are locked into reification tend to deny evidence that challenges their belief. While Xerox should be a good enough example for any for-profit company, the naysayers will counter with: "Well, we don't make photocopiers here, so that doesn't apply to us!" Find the example that is so close to home that it cannot be denied.

In education, provide examples of other schools or colleges that took a proactive stance and have been able to change their destiny. The Koality Kids program with the American Society for Quality Control is an excellent example of educators being proactive and taking the initiative to use the quality discipline in the education field. They are using participative methods to involve parents and the community in the school system and applying tools such as quality function deployment to the operation of the school system.

At the university level, look at the mechanical engineering department of the University of Wisconsin–Madison. This organization used quality function deployment to redesign their engineering curriculum.[1] Or, you can examine the University of North Carolina–Charlotte's quality steering committee and total quality effort.[2]

In the service sector, give illustrations of service groups that charted a course and stayed on that course to become successful. For example, look at the success of the Bethesda Naval Hospital in using a quality emphasis to solve organiza-

---

1. Donald S. Ermer, "Using Quality Function Deployment Becomes an Educational Experience for Students and Faculty," *Quality Progress* Vol. 28, Number 5 (May 1995), 131–136.

2. Kimberly Buch and J. William Shelnutt, "University of North Carolina-Charlotte Measures the Effects of Its Quality Initiative," *Quality Progress* Vol. 28, Number 7 (July 1995), 73–77.

tional problems. They developed a macro flowchart of processes, benchmarked their activities, and used teams to identify and solve problems, collect data, and track progress. While working in a military environment, they flattened their hierarchy to involve all major components of the organization, including finance, nursing, and the supply organization.[3]

In government, look at the case studies of cities, counties, and states that have become proactive and progressed in solving their problems. The Minnesota Department of Transportation is a leader in fostering strategic change based on a quality revolution. Their employee quality teams have improved dozens of processes such as how to patch potholes and improve snow removal. The City of Saint Paul created an employee Quality Council that leads the quality efforts throughout city government. Most branches of the city have employee teams using quality tools to improve their services. All the government agencies in Minnesota cooperate together hosting a statewide quality conference to further the quality revolution in state government.

Witnessing other people winning in situations similar to yours is the best way to overcome reification, accompanied by effective skills to accomplish the planning. To overcome and avoid reification, you may have to wage a war of information (see Figure 5.3).

Figure 5.3.   Waging the Information Campaign

- Use articles from professional journals.
- Send people to conferences.
- Benchmark best practices.
- Provide training that focuses on proactive and participative leadership.
- Invite managers to attend professional society meetings.
- Bring in videotapes on quality.
- Utilize a local college to organize workshops on quality.

---

3. Kaye Appleman and Kris Large, "Navy Hospital Fights Disease with a Quality Team," *Quality Progress* Vol. 28, Number 4 (April 1995), 47–49.

Educated Incapacity

While some people suffer from the belief that it is not possible to create change, others suffer from the desire to overanalyze situations and ignore the basic actions that can be taken to improve a situation.

In many organizations there are individuals who are well-educated but unable to take action. Their education may have emphasized compiling lots of data before making a decision and placed a high value on research to confirm any decision. Some of these individuals are paralyzed when the time comes to make a decision. They ignore common-sense answers to problems because there is no evidence that can be run through a super computer.

Herman Kahn, the futurist, called this condition "educated incapacity." Kahn observed that "education necessarily involves selection, indoctrination, a special intellectual environment, the development of a framework of accepted 'givens' or 'facts,' and learning to think about a subject in a certain required way."[4] This learned way of thinking about issues can often inhibit innovative thinking or common sense that may be necessary to solve a problem.

Many organizations suffer from "the paralysis of analysis," when too much analysis is required before a decision can be rendered. While decision making based on data is an important virtue, it can be carried to excess. These excesses tend to create the situation observed by Kahn.

In a recent motion picture, *Willow,* a village shaman casts a set of bones on the ground to divine what should be done to solve a problem. The shaman looks at the bones and whispers to the main character, "The bones tell me nothing." From there he has to use his best judgment to solve the prob-

---

4. Herman Kahn, *Things to Come* (Macmillan Co., 1972), 28.

lem. We should always try to find data that will help us make rational decisions, but sometimes the bones will tell us nothing. In those cases we must be prepared to use our best judgment and common sense. In these situations, people must fall back on their consensus-based mission and vision and their understanding of the organization's values.

Educated incapacity is seen most often when a group of people are gathered into a team. The members represent all the major parts of the organization and were selected to serve on the team because they have a good grasp of what is going on in the organization. They are, for all practical purposes, a representative sample of the organization. In their desire to make sound decisions these teams often decide that they need to conduct a survey to find out what everyone in the organization thinks about an issue. If they would trust their own knowledge, they often would find that they already know the answers to their survey questions.

It *is* important to use data and not rely just on hunches. But the collection of data has an economic cost for any organization. All statistical data is organized to provide a certain degree of confidence in the reliability of the data. In many cases, people trap themselves by desiring a much higher level of confidence in their data than the situation warrants. A representative sample, such as a group of people, can give sound data without surveying 100 percent of the people in the organization.

Another form of educated incapacity can be seen in people who are taught to be a manager based upon a single understanding of how an organization is structured. This is often reinforced by the curriculum of business schools that only prepare managers to lead within a narrow range of leadership options. When market efficiency forces managers to become more participative in their leadership styles, they are inhibited because of what they learned in the past.

Deming argued that most of the problems in American industry were due to the thinking and practices taught in our business schools. Fortunately, some business schools now support the quality revolution and are beginning to contribute to the theoretical framework.

Self-fulfilling Prophecies

It was said in the nineteenth century that the eagle of the United States would spread her wings from the Atlantic to the Pacific. This statement of the country's destiny became a self-fulfilling prophecy because many people decided to act individually based upon the vision, and their collective actions caused the prophecy to come true.

Self-fulfilling prophecy has been shown to be a real phenomenon in a variety of circumstances. Rumors of weakness in a financial institution cause people to withdraw their investments, making the institution weak. Telling a child that he or she is a poor student causes the child to perform as such. Merely telling people that they are producing poor quality materials can cause them to accept poor quality as normal, assuring that low quality is all they will ever produce.

There are certain assumptions or statements that can become self-fulfilling prophecies in organizations. For example, regarding the roles of a union and management, each side can have low expectations for the other that become real based on the way they approach each other. This is a significant issue in organizations where employees are represented by bargaining units.

If managers have an expectation that employees will not care about quality, then management will act on that assumption and probably do things that encourage employees not to care about quality. On the other hand, when management believes that quality is an essential ingredient in the organization's success, then managers start taking actions that will turn this belief into reality. Of course, simply hoping for quality in an organization does not create quality. However, people's expectations cause them to take actions that will make the expectations become real, and that is why the self-fulfilling prophecy concept must be understood.

For example, consider the performance of Habitat For Humanity. Here is an organization that takes on a seemingly impossible goal—the elimination of poverty housing—does their work with volunteer labor, and achieves some of the highest quality work in the home construction industry. How do they do it? This is self-fulfilling prophecy at work. Habitat staff and volunteers believe they can accomplish a mission that most people would not even attempt to fulfill. They have a vision about what they want to achieve and they place a high value on quality.

Habitat's commitment to building quality homes was put to the test when hurricane Andrew swept through southern Florida a few years ago. Acre upon acre of housing projects were flattened by this massive storm, except for the Habitat homes. Why? They chose housing designs and used construction methods that made quality their highest priority. Whether a house was blitz-built or put up over several months, all the houses were built using hurricane clips with the roof trusses and correct nailing of shingles so that high winds could not penetrate them.

Scan the Horizon

The members of the planning team share a common understanding by reviewing the past and are ready to focus their attention on the forces surrounding the organization that will influence its future. This is the process of scanning the horizon.

The planning team has a concept of the organization's destination, based on the customer's input. The team understands the history that shaped its current situation from using the time line exercise, and how to function internally based on the statement of values. Now the team must ask about the other forces that will impact their planning. Other forces may include competition, government regulations, demographic trends, inflation, elections, anticipated technical breakthroughs, as well as social trends.

To deny the impact of the external forces is like planning a ski vacation without anticipating the level of snowfall. The scanning process includes the knowledge obtained by listening to the voice of the customer, as well as consideration of what the competition is doing, and other financial, market, technological, and societal factors.

Figure 5.4. Consider the External Forces

What	Why	How
Identify the factors outside and inside the organization that will impact the ability to accomplish the mission.	When recognized, plans can be made to utilize or mitigate the influence of external and internal forces.	Force field analysis.

One tool used to organize this scanning process is the force field analysis, introduced by Kurt Lewin, a social scientist. The force field analysis allows people to visually display the various forces that will impact a situation positively or negatively. For planning purposes, it is important to identify the forces that will help you achieve your overall objective, and those that will hinder you. These forces can be written on an easel pad as a chart for everyone in the planning group to see. Such a chart will look like Figure 5.5.

With these forces identified, the actions that will be taken to strengthen or build on the supporting forces and to weaken or counteract the hindering forces can be identified. For example, suppose you are conducting a strategic plan for

Figure 5.5.　Force Field Analysis Chart

Forces that support our objective		Forces that hinder our objective
_____ >	< _____
_____ >	< _____
_____ >	< _____
_____ >	< _____

a community college. What forces would impact your plan? A supporting force would be the availability of well-qualified part-time instructors from local businesses. A hindering force would be the increasing cost of new books needed to keep the school's library at a point where it can meet accreditation.

Figure 5.6.　Force Field Analysis for a Community College's Strategic Plan

Forces that support quality		Forces that challenge quality
Available instructors from local businesses.	>	< Increased cost of new books and periodicals.
Availability of statewide resources, such as a state-level quality awards program.	>	< Traditional reluctance to partner with business.
Increased number of high school graduates with high GPAs.	>	< Competition for best students.

What actions can be taken to strengthen the college's reputation based on the part-time instructors? One action would be for local businesses to advertise the college courses on their bulletin boards, emphasizing the experience and qualifications of the instructors. What can be done to diminish the impact of increasing costs for the library? One option would be to create a specific endowment fund for the library that will attract new support from the community.

Define Your Objectives

Accomplishing the mission of the organization requires that many specific objectives be identified by the strategic planning team. Some of these objectives will come from the external force field analysis, such as those identified in the community college example. Others will come from looking at the internal forces in the organization such as aging facilities, employee suggestions, environmental legacies, and new inventions.

The process of identifying the specific objectives for the plan involves asking and answering a question: "What are the objectives we need to accomplish to achieve our mission and vision, based upon our values and the forces impacting our organization?" Or, to put it more succinctly, ask the people in the group what they think the organization must do to get where it wants to be in the future. The answer to this question depends on the people who are involved in the analysis and their perceptions of the issues. There is no "right" answer.

For large organizations, these objectives can be grouped together in categories for ease of documentation and to give a better, comprehensive picture of how the objectives intertwine. For example, a small city government conducted a strategy session in which several major categories of objectives were identified for improving the quality of the community. The planning team consisted of elected commissioners; professional staff from the police, fire, parks and economic development departments; and leaders from local business; the superintendent of schools; a dean from the local college; and chairpersons from neighborhood committees.

The team reviewed the forces impacting the community through a force field analysis. They conducted a time line exercise to create a level playing field and common set of perspectives about how the current situation came to be. The planning team identified three key objectives for their strategic plan. These were:

1. Restore human development qualities to the neighborhoods.

2. Reduce and ultimately eliminate poverty.
3. Restore the housing stock to excellent condition while providing affordable housing opportunities for all.

One major objective dealt with reducing and eliminating poverty. Under this category were several enabling actions, such as providing education, training, and resources to succeed; strengthening existing businesses; and providing resources for new and existing businesses. So each objective can be broken down into specific enabling actions, which can be illustrated with a traditional Ishikawa, or cause-and-effect, diagram as shown in Figure 5.7.

Figure 5.7.   Enabling Actions

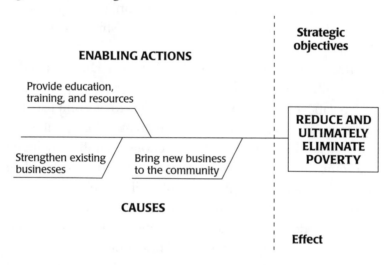

Under "education, training, and resources to succeed" were several specific enabling actions, such as eliminating high school dropouts, unifying and marketing work force preparedness programs, providing day care programs to trainees and newly employed parents, providing medical care to the uninsured, and bolstering public transportation so low-income people could afford to get to work.

Figure 5.8. Education, Training, and Resources

The specific tactics that support each enabling action can be illustrated with the Ishikawa diagram in Figure 5.8. Each tactic can then be developed as a plan, with steps, deadlines, and people accountable for accomplishing the plan on schedule.

In another example, a local Habitat For Humanity affiliate identified a broad strategic objective that required several specific enabling actions in order to accomplish the objective. The objective was to increase the number of houses being built. The enabling actions identified included expanding the number of churches committed to building homes, increasing the number of skilled volunteers who could serve as construction supervisors, expanding the mailing list for donors, adding more fund-raising events, and enhancing the group's ability to identify potential homeowners for the program. Success in all of the actions would enable the organization to achieve its objective and fulfill its mission (see Figure 5.9).

In an industrial setting, a Lockheed Martin factory identified several broad objectives, such as lowering production costs, achieving operational excellence, and constantly improving its standards of quality as vital to achieving its mission

Figure 5.9. Enabling Actions for Strategic Objectives

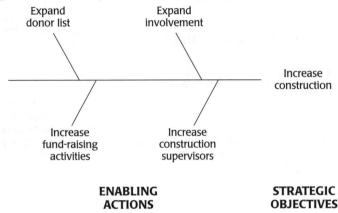

Expand
donor list

Expand
involvement

Increase
construction

Increase
fund-raising
activities

Increase
construction
supervisors

**ENABLING
ACTIONS**

**STRATEGIC
OBJECTIVES**

and vision. Their mission was well-defined: to produce a commodity. Their vision was to be the lowest cost, highest quality producer of this commodity and thereby become the preferred source in the world market. As Figure 5.10 shows, the mission and vision of the industrial company is supported by three key strategic objectives.

Specific enabling actions are then identified to support each overarching objective. In the quality area, actions included items such as ensuring that products and services would meet or exceed pre-established levels of acceptance;

Figure 5.10. Highest Quality, Lowest Cost Producer

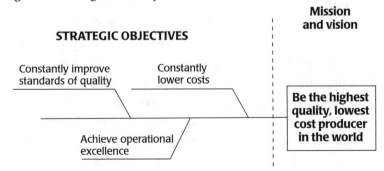

**Mission
and vision**

STRATEGIC OBJECTIVES

Constantly improve
standards of quality

Constantly
lower costs

**Be the highest
quality, lowest
cost producer
in the world**

Achieve operational
excellence

Figure 5.11. Enabling Actions

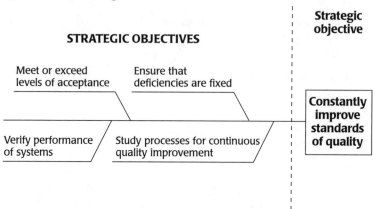

ensuring that deficiencies in the quality program are fixed; verification of the performance of systems, components, activities, and services; and systematic study of processes for continuous improvement. Accomplishment of each action would allow the facility to achieve its objectives and succeed in its mission. Figure 5.11 illustrates the relationship of the enabling actions to their strategic objective.

The Planning Horizon

How far into the future should the strategic plan reach? When the planning team is creating its vision of what the successful future will look like, how many years ahead should they project?

The answer to this question lies in the movement of ships at sea. Small ships can maneuver in a short amount of time and space. Large ships require a lot more forethought, time, and space to be able to change directions.

For-profit companies that have tough competition should look seven to ten years into the future; this is far enough ahead to keep the organization focused on realistic change. Small-scale technical change comes so fast that projecting beyond a decade will often be of little value. On the other hand, some companies in high technology fields, such as defense, computing, and telecommunications, are obviously making mergers and acquisitions that are intended to provide market advantages over multiple decades.

Long-term institutions, like hospitals, schools, and power utilities should project at least twenty years into the future, and in some cases fifty years. Tokyo Electric Power Company, for example, conducts its strategic planning with a fifty-year time horizon. The technical changes that will affect long-term institutions are often relatively easy to predict, such as the planned implementation of fusion power. Demographic information for schools, hospitals, and other institutions is readily available to support a twenty-year projection. Social, political, and economic factors may have an impact in the short term. For example, the healthcare industry is experiencing restructuring to accommodate new levels of cost-cutting and competitiveness, and utilities are faced with deregulation. These types of forces create the need for short- and medium-term adaptability *within* a long-range strategic plan. City governments should likewise develop their future projections based on at least twenty years, possibly longer. Unlike businesses, cities do not tend to go out of business. Some have lasted for 3,000 years already.

Confusing Objectives with Alternatives

The world is full of alternatives in search of objectives. If you set foot on a car lot, you will see hundreds of alternatives from which you can choose. How will you decide which car is the best one for you? The answer to this question is that the best car for you is the one that meets your objectives. What do you want this vehicle to do for you? What are the objectives you want to achieve with this car? Selection of an alternative based on objectives is the sound way to do business.

In the quality arena, there are a multitude of alternatives available for helping organizations to improve. It is very good that there are so many alternatives, except when people mistake these alternatives for objectives. Implementing statistical process control is not an objective for an organization. It is an alternative—a path that can be taken to achieve an objective. Utilizing self-managed work teams is not an objective, but it is an alternative that might help an organization succeed.

The reason that so many companies are trying so many different approaches to quality, such as design of experiments, statistical process control, cross-functional teams, and zero defects, (and thereby creating the perception that these methods are just passing fads) is that the organization lacks a clear understanding of the objectives they are trying to achieve when one of these alternatives is utilized.

Strategic planning allows organizations to avoid this pitfall by carefully focusing on strategic objectives and the enabling actions necessary for success. The alternatives that are selected as action items to meet the strategic and enabling actions will be in their proper supportive role and can be evaluated based on their effectiveness.

Agree to Organize Around the Objectives

At this stage in the strategic planning process, a list of key objectives should be prepared and everyone on the planning team should achieve a consensus that these key objectives are the right ones upon which to focus energy and attention. Consensus can be established through dialogue or through a structured decision-making tool like nominal group technique.

Multiple Scenarios

In preparing to develop specific action plans to accomplish the enabling actions in the strategic plan, the team may find an advantage in using multiple scenarios of the future. The team can envision scenarios based on the possibility of events going well for the organization, going very badly, and going in a manner that most of the team thinks is likely to happen.

Using multiple scenarios offers advantages. An optimistic scenario can be developed, in which planners anticipate everything that might go right and make plans based on how to build on good fortune. A pessimistic scenario can be developed to anticipate how the future will unfold if most events do not go well for the organization, while a middle-of-the-road scenario can establish expectations for a future in which some things go well and others do not.

Having various outcomes offers the advantage of allowing people to assess events as they happen and then move quickly to evaluate their impact and better understand their ramifications. Branch points can be identified ahead of time that indicate when decisions must be made or when compensatory actions must be taken, if the pessimistic scenario starts to unfold in real life. Or, if events are more successful, the scenario can help people assess when it is time to launch new actions to take advantage of successes.

The use of multiple scenarios allows the organization to fully recognize the potential problems as well as future opportunities. Often, people will create only an optimistic scenario because they don't recognize that things can go wrong, or they do not want to admit that failure is a possibility. The inability to recognize what might go wrong is a major contribution to poor quality in many organizations.

For example, the planning task force for a city government decided to create several scenarios to identify the actions they would take to achieve their mission and their strategic objectives. One scenario was generated around the possibility that no additional funding would be forthcoming and that whatever was to be done would be done with the existing resources. A second scenario considered the possibilities of actions that could be taken given a modest increase in funding. The objectives to be accomplished were the same, but the possibility of more funding broadened the list of potential actions. A third scenario was developed based on the possibility of major federal funding under the Empowerment Zone legislation. This scenario addressed the same issues as the other two, but offered a wide range of actions that would be possible with major funding.

Strategic Objective:
Restore human development qualities to neighborhoods

Items from scenario 1: No additional funding

- Strengthen partnerships for joint jurisdictional law enforcement training.
- Train crime prevention volunteers.
- Form partnerships for comprehensive neighborhood meetings.
- Bolster existing weed and trash programs.
- Establish community group to evaluate abandoned buildings for potential re-use.
- Institute neighborhood leadership training program.
- Evaluate mini-park facility needs.
- Establish panel to coordinate volunteer services.

Items from scenario 2: Modest funding increases

- Provide drug education for fourth, fifth, and sixth graders.
- Place additional officers in highest crime zone.

- Add two people to reinstitute building code enforcement.
- Expand services of family resource centers.
- Expand afterschool programs to target at-risk youth.
- Expand Boys Club and Girls Club program.

Items from scenario 3: Major funding available

- Thirty additional police cruisers for Take-Home car program.
- Re-use program for community centerpiece buildings.
- Construct new community centerpiece buildings.
- Improve Boys Club and Girls Club facilities.
- Fund mini-parks improvement program.
- Implement afterschool program at all city schools.

Identifying the Gaps

When the objectives are agreed upon, and various scenarios are considered that might affect how they are achieved, the planning team will focus next on the gaps that exist between where the organization presently stands and where it needs to be.

Baldrige and ISO 9000 Notes

Baldrige examiners want to know how an organization conducts its scanning process and look for evidence that this step has occurred prior to the establishment of objectives. The key objectives illustrated in Figure 5.7 would be called the "key business drivers" in Baldrige terminology.

The establishment of key quality-related objectives is a major step in ISO 9000. Based on these objectives, an organization may choose to emphasize specific parts of the overall quality management system. Most ISO 9000 practitioners are familiar with some form of "gap analysis" described in this chapter.

Chapter Notes

The concept of reification has been advanced by adult educators such as Paulo Freire and Stephen Brookfield.

The concept of multiple scenarios in planning, along with "educated incapacity, was articulated by Dr. Herman Kahn, founder of the Hudson Institute for the Study of the Future.

Chapter 6

Closing the Gaps

"Are we there yet?"
My kids

When you go on a journey, you start by identifying the destination you want to reach. Then you figure out how far away that place is and what you have to do to get there.

The same thing is true in strategic planning. The planning team identifies the goals that need to be achieved in order to assure high quality in whatever the endeavor may be. Then, the team determines how large a gap exists between the current situation and the goal and decides how to best close the gap.

Sometimes organizations fail to assess the size of the gap. This can lead to some serious problems, such as underestimating the difficulty of the journey or overkilling the issue. Organizations often have the elements in place that can greatly improve their performance, but in their zeal for improvement they overlook their current strengths and pursue new programs, causing people to lose enthusiasm about supporting organizational objectives. In other cases, people believe that they can create genuine change merely by employing propaganda methods; this can lead to cynicism among the members of the organization. The size of the gap must be estimated in order to prepare a plan for reaching the goal.

Figure 6.1.   Plan to Close the Gaps

What	Why	How
Develop a plan to close the gaps between each goal and the "as is" current situation.	Without a specific agreed-upon plan, there will be no progress in improving quality.	Determine difficulty level and importance of each gap.
		Identify quality tool(s) to use that will help close each gap.

When an organization has many actions to perform, it helps to have some method to compare the relative difficulty of each action. There is no best way to do this. One way is to ask people to consider which of the actions will be easy to accomplish, which will be very difficult, and which will fall in the middle between these extremes. The relative difficulty of accomplishing the actions may be roughly categorized as high, medium, and low.

The relative importance of each action should also be considered while people are thinking about how to close the gaps between the existing condition and the desired condition. Obviously all of the actions should be of some importance, or else they would not show up as enabling actions that support strategic objectives. However, some will be more critical to the organization's success than others. They can be categorized in three levels: actions that are essential to the organization, actions that are important to achieve, and actions that would be nice to have but the organization can survive without at least for now.

It is possible to put these two ideas together to get a useful perspective of the actions, showing their relative importance and their relative difficulty, together. Using the example of the volunteer agency building houses in the previous chapter, we might assess their goals to look like those in Figure 6.2.

Figure 6.2. Levels of Importance and Difficulty

Actions	Relative Importance	Relative Difficulty
1. Find volunteers to help with construction.	Medium	Low
2. Approach corporations for major donations.	High	Medium
3. Design and implement a fund-raising schedule.	Medium	Medium
4. Find a volunteer construction supervisor.	High	High
5. Expand the mailing list.	Low	Low

This exercise helps people assess the amount of energy they are going to have to put into accomplishing their actions. In this example, finding a volunteer construction supervisor is apparently not going to be easy, and it is essential to have this person or the houses cannot be built. The gap here is large and the organization needs to focus attention on this immediately. Expanding the mailing list, on the other hand, will be a good thing to do this year, but houses will be built regardless of whether or not this task is done. Finding more names can be done easily by borrowing the mailing lists of other area agencies.

Clearly the organization should put its best resources to work on finding a volunteer construction supervisor, and the progress of this action should be regularly monitored. How does this relate to quality? The organization knows that an experienced construction supervisor is the key to good, efficient, and safe building practices. Without this person in place, the quality of the final product will suffer greatly, along with the reputation of the organization.

Assessing the relative importance and relative difficulty of each gap between the "should" and the actual enables people to direct their energy for closing the gaps. Deciding how to close the gaps requires some creative energy and a variety of perspectives.

Figure 6.3.　Closing the Gaps

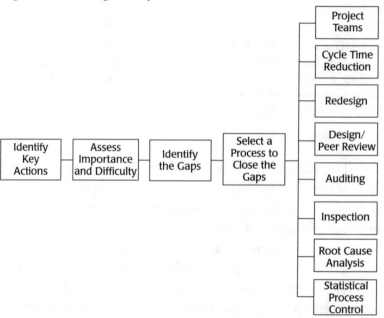

For those who are working heavily in the ISO 9000 framework, closing the gaps can be thought of as identifying the process improvements that need to occur. This could be a direct work process, an inspection or verification process, or an administrative process.

While the concept of closing the gaps may sound lengthy—given the detail provided on methods in this chapter—the actual selection process for determining which gaps need attention often takes less than an hour for a team to accomplish.

Deciding How to Close the Gaps

Let's stay with the illustration of the volunteers who are building community housing for a moment. They decide that it is imperative to recruit a couple of volunteers to supervise construction. This is the most important gap they need to close this year in order to fulfill their mission and maintain their standard of quality. How are they going to find these volunteers?

If the strategic planning is being carried out by two or three people, then the ideas for recruiting these volunteers are limited to the experience and creativity of the two or three people who are making the plan, unless they appoint a committee. They would do very well to give this assignment to a team with people who bring a variety of points of view and experiences to the issue. Then, based on the combined knowledge and creativity of this team, a better plan can be developed for finding the volunteers.

The great strength of the project team approach is the combined knowledge, experience, insights, and creativity of a group of people when they are brought together to resolve a problem, equipped with the right analysis tools. A larger group will probably create a greater pool of ideas, with good chances that one of these ideas will provide the best possible solution to a problem.

It is extremely important in any planning endeavor to involve in the creation of the plan the people who must implement the plan. Plans that are created by people who do not have the day-to-day knowledge of the process can be off-target and waste a great deal of time and energy.

Using the Quality Tools to Close the Gap

While organizations should embrace quality as an essential ingredient in their mission and values, the specific tools such as project teams, cycle time reduction, process redesign, auditing, root cause analysis, and statistical process control, enable them to achieve their quality objectives. The mere *use* of the tools should not be an objective for an organization. Instead, the organization needs to use the right tool to get the job done. The right tool will depend on the nature of the job to be performed.

Let's take a look at some of the standard quality tools, and a few that have entered the quality field from some other areas, to see how they can help organizations close the quality gaps and achieve their strategic goals.

Project by Project Continuous Improvement

Often, organizations identify goals that relate to reducing costs or making customers more satisfied with products and services. In many instances, there are plenty of opportunities for cost savings and improved customer satisfaction that can be accomplished through the use of many small project teams.

The project team idea was systematically defined and advocated by Juran, who noted that improvements do not simply happen in an organization, but only occur when people get organized to cause them to occur.

For project teams to work effectively in an organization, they need to have boundaries established by management. Within these boundaries, team members are free to gather information, make decisions, and implement new ideas. If a team needs resources or wants to take actions that will impact people or systems outside its boundaries, the team needs to negotiate these issues with management.

One of the appeals of project teams is that the teams are usually effective at eliminating waste or scrap from work processes. Most people support this type of effort. Usually, the only people who resist these efforts are those who have been managing the process and who do not want to have to admit that there is waste and inefficiency in the system that they did not ferret out themselves.

Figure 6.4. Guidelines for Forming Effective Project Teams

- Ensure that all impacted groups are represented on the team.
- Clearly define the scope and boundaries of the team's work.
- Establish a time frame for completion.
- Ensure that team members have diagnostic skills.
- Empower the team to implement ideas.

The drawback with project teams is that there is often a need to make a considerable investment in training team members to use the basic quality tools in order to harness the opportunities for improvement that exist. Fundamentally, this problem will persist until the organization's work force is fully trained.

> Example: A manufacturing plant uses power transformers in the operation of motors in its production process. The transformers need cleaning to remain efficient. Old methods are no longer allowable under OSHA rules. A team that included people from the plant's maintenance, engineering, safety, and industrial hygiene organizations studied the problem and designed a new piece of equipment and process for cleaning transformers. The team's efforts provided improved efficiency worth $200,000 a year in production capacity.

Cycle Time Reduction

One of the quality tools used by project teams is the flow diagram, which defines the sequence in which tasks are done in a work system. Defining the flow of a process allows the organization to identify obvious barriers to efficient performance. Once the flow is defined, the amount of time required by each step, as well as the amount of rework in the step and even the real need for the step, can be analyzed with an eye to streamlining.

Reducing the cycle time is often a key enabling force in closing an organization's gaps between its desired and actual states, as long as the quality of the process is maintained. Whether it is designing a new computer, cooking a hamburger, processing students' applications, assessing a medical condition, or responding to a citizen's call for police assistance, shortening the time for accomplishing a task often gives an organization a competitive service advantage and impresses the customers.

Figure 6.5.   Steps in Cycle Time Reduction

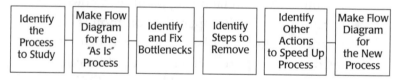

The drawback to cycle time reduction is that it can be threatening to people in an organization. The process dredges up memories of efficiency experts timing people with stop watches and looking for the perfect amount of coal to be shoveled every minute. People sometimes perceive that cycle time reduction experts are brought in to fix a system without first giving them an opportunity to fix their system internally.

The advantage of bringing in an expert is that this person has experience with process flow analysis and can help an organization avoid pitfalls.

Example: In order to meet OSHA requirements, a production plant began issuing its
employees respirators for protection from
chemicals. The process for cleaning and reis-
suing respirators was very slow, causing the
production staff to buy more and more respirators in order to stay in compliance and keep
work on schedule. A study of the respirator
cleaning process identified a bottleneck that
was changed. Other improvements helped cut
the overall cycle time down to one-fourth of
the earlier time required. The timely delivery
of the respirators meant that the production
group avoided the purchase of new respirators for several years.

Redesigning Systems

Continuous improvement project teams and cycle time
reduction teams share many common features. Both harness the knowledge of the workforce, using systematic
methods of data collection to redesign a work system. This
form of system redesign can be effective as a grass-roots
change strategy and takes on even more power when linked
to an organization's strategic plan. Combining top-down
leadership of process redesign through a strategic plan
with the local grass-roots initiatives for continuous
improvement has proven to be extremely successful for
many organizations.

Ken Gadd and John Oakland have found that organizations that have been successful with participatory systems
redesign, driven by quality-centered strategic plans, can effectively expand their redesign efforts into larger-scale reengineering of major work systems that lead to changes in the

organization's structure.[1] They emphasize, however, that process reengineering should be focused on improving core processes that are central to the organization's strategy of aligning work processes with customers' requirements.

Hammer and Champy have described this reengineering as "the fundamental rethinking and radical redesign of business processes to achieve dramatic improvements in critical, contemporary measures such as cost, quality, service, and speed."[2]

In essence, business process reengineering expands the role of a continuous improvement team by charging a team with responsibility for wholesale redesign that may include changing the organization chart. A team is chartered to utilize a broad array of tools, including benchmarking and consideration of the most up-to-date information technology, to innovate, re-think, reorganize, and retool the targeted part of the organization. The end-product should be a very different organization, often using new technology, that achieves a breakthrough in efficiency, quality, and reduced cost. The steps in this process are outlined in Figure 6.6.

While new technology is not always the source of breakthrough in reengineering, many of the best examples have been based on the introduction of new technology into a system. New information technology, such as expert systems, the use of the Internet, distance learning, and shared databases give organizations new tools for accomplishing their objectives.

However, numerous attempts to launch business process reengineering have not been based on a quality centered strategic plan. These efforts have often occurred in organiza-

---

1. Ken W. Gadd and John S. Oakland, "Chimera or Culture? Business Process Reengineering for Total Quality Management," *Quality Management Journal* vol 3, no. 3 (1996), 20.

2. Michael Hammer and James Champy, *Reengineering the Corporation: A Manifesto for Business Revolution* (New York: Harper Business, 1993), 32.

Figure 6.6. Steps in Business Process Redesign

1. Identify the process to be reengineered based on the goals of the strategic plan.
2. Organize and charter a team to conduct the reengineering.
3. Gather data by conducting benchmarking and assessing the possible use of new information technology.
4. Redesign the business operation based on the collection of data and input from the current status of the system.
5. Conduct a trial to prove that the redesign will work.
6. Develop a plan for implementation that includes preparing people for the change, rewriting procedures, obtaining, and installing new equipment.
7. Obtain senior management approval to implement the plan.
8. Implement the redesign.

tions that have not valued quality as a core principle in their mission statement and have failed in many case studies. The fault lies not in the concept and the tools of reengineering, but with those who have sought to create what Deming has called "instant pudding."

Organizations that begin with a quality-centered focus on mission, vision, and a customer-driven strategic plan will have the right foundation for sponsoring both the small-scale system redesign achieved by project teams and cycle time reduction, and the major systems reengineering efforts.

> Example: For decades, the design and manufacture of precision machined parts for a defense program involved hand-drawn designs being prepared in one part of the country that were sent to another region where the designs were studied and numerical controls were developed for precision machine tools. In a major system reengineering effort, a new "art to part" system was created that allowed the designer's work to be transfered directly to the machine that would fabricate the equipment. This redesign created tremendous cost savings, shortened the cycle

time for fabrication, and made many changes in the organization structure.

Design and Peer Review

The literature that focuses on quality improvement often overlooks the traditional tools of quality control. However, in some cases the control of work can be a vital tool in achieving the organization's quality goals.

In the professional field, the process of peer review is a reliable tool to help ensure quality products and services. Research scientists, for instance, rely heavily on the opinion of their peers to determine what is good science and what is poor research. The medical field likewise relies on the "second opinion" as a form of ensuring the quality of decisions. Peer review can play an important role in ensuring the quality of legal opinions, social work practices, and many types of work in the volunteer sector.

Figure 6.7. Elements of Peer Review

1. Establish a policy and process.
   - When should review occur?
   - Who is qualified to review?
   - What are the limits of reviews?
2. Implement the process.
   - Communicate the policy and process.
   - Track level of activity.
   - Verify that reviews occur.
3. Evaluate the process.
   - Is it timely?
   - Does it accomplish its purpose?
   - How can it be improved?

Many professionals, such as engineers, computer scientists, and architects will utilize the process of design review, in which a person other than the original designer reviews the work that has been done to ensure that appropriate and accurate calculations and assessments have been made.

> Example: A municipal government identified training problems as a major gap in achieving their quality goals. A team from human resources reviewed the guidelines for conducting new employee training and on-the-job training. Supervisors identified as effective trainers were asked to sit in on training conducted by fellow supervisors, review their training, critique it, and help make improvements.

Auditing

Some things are so important that the organization must build in a mechanism to ensure that the work is performed correctly. For instance, the distribution of controlled substances in a hospital, the control of nuclear fuel in a power plant, and the maintenance of aircraft engines at an airline are all of critical importance to the safety of customers, employees, and the general public. In these situations, organizations must design periodic quality audits for their processes and procedures to make absolutely sure that deviations do not creep into the system.

The use of audits is one of the most expensive methods for assuring quality, so audits need to be shrewdly planned and only utilized in the most important circumstances. Over-reliance on audits means unnecessary costs for the organization. An under-reliance on audits creates the potential for undetected deviations in critical systems where the organization cannot afford any failures.

The most important areas for incorporating audits involve the health and safety of employees. Safety systems should be audited to ensure they are adequate and that they perform as expected. The peer review process may need to be audited to ensure that it has not been compromised by people who are willing to take excessive risks to meet deadlines or quotas. Audits are often used to ensure that the quality of purchased materials has not been compromised and that financial systems are reporting accurate data.

Figure 6.8. Elements of an Effective Audit Program

- Recruit or train qualified auditors.
- Clearly identify the reason and scope of audits.
- Clearly identify the criteria against which audits will be conducted.
- Provide adequate time for audit preparation, performance, and review.
- Establish commitment to address audit findings.
- Maintain documentation of the audit.

Of course no one likes to be audited. It makes people uncomfortable. Some people consider the audit to be a statement that they are not trusted by the organization. An audit program needs to clearly express the intent that audits are conducted because the audited tasks are critical to the quality of the organization's products or services.

> Example: A manufacturing firm generated a variety of waste products that required special planning and handling in order to comply with federal and state codes. The strategic plan identified 100 percent compliance as a vital step in achieving the firm's overall quality objectives. An audit program was established, using the codes as the audit criteria. A special audit function was created, separate from the

line organization and the waste management group, to assess the degree of compliance to the codes. Over time, the rigorous audit process helped the organization achieve consistent 100 percent compliance to requirements.

There is also an entirely different kind of audit in which a program is audited instead of the performance of a specific system or process. Programmatic audits usually allow an outside party to evaluate an overall program, such as quality management, environmental management, or financial management. As part of the organization's plan to ensure quality, there may be a desire or a requirement to submit to a programmatic audit to obtain or maintain certification, such as ISO 9000 certification or a college accreditation board approval, or to meet the requirements of a parent company. In some cases, a government agency such as NASA will require a programmatic audit of a vendor's quality program to ensure that a systematic approach to quality exists in the vendor's organization.

Inspections

In most cases, the use of statistical data, and the random sampling of incoming or outgoing materials, can give an organization the assurance of quality needed to meet organizational objectives.

There are some places where the potential cost of failure is too high to rely on statistical data. There are situations where an organization will choose to rely on 100 percent inspection in order to meet goals and accomplish the mission. Examples of this approach include the assurance of the welds in nuclear reactors and the preflight inspection of aircraft.

Figure 6.9.   Elements of an Effective Inspection Program

- Define criteria for acceptance (e.g., national standards, quality attributes).
- Establish a statistically valid sampling plan.
- Train qualified inspectors.
- Establish appropriate records system.
- Assure independence of inspectors.
- Track and trend results.
- Use results to improve the process.

Example: A school system established a fire protection program as part of its efforts to upgrade the quality of the school facilities. One component of the fire protection program involved ensuring that fire extinguishers were in place and kept fully charged. A sampling schedule was created and an inspector was identified to affirm that the extinguishers were in place and charged throughout the year.

Self-Assessments

Self-assessments are another tool of the quality professional that can be applied to achieve the major objectives in a strategic plan. For key areas of the plan, managers can conduct their own assessment of the quality performance of their organization.

A self-assessment is a formal and structured process of examining specific data to determine whether or not an organization is on track in conducting work properly and achieving quality results. The organization's quality manager usually works with the line management to identify the appropriate data that needs to be included in the self-assessment. This may include checksheets on operational log books, team-level performance indicators, control charts from important processes, or action plans that the organization has committed to fulfill.

The managers bring together the leadership team, along with appropriate employee representatives, and review all the data. After all the information has been digested, the group determines which performance areas are strong and which are weak. If, for example, a review of the log books shows that process samples were not always being taken for analysis, then the situation needs to be corrected by exploring why the samples were not obtained. The group should make a list of the areas that need more attention or effort and make new plans to improve.

Self-assessment offers managers many advantages over audits. First, it is easier to own up to a problem when you find it yourself. Second, there is still time to fix the problem on your own. Third, self-assessment can help drive out fear and create a climate where continuous improvement becomes a real value, if conducted properly. Of course, if the self-assessment leads to assigning blame instead of fixing problems, it will backfire as a process for driving out fear.

> Example: The officers in a fire department planned a self-assessment exercise as a major component of their continuous improvement quality process. They assembled data that gave evidence regarding their frequency of verification of fire extinguishers and walk-down of fire water systems. They shared results from inspection of their fire fighting equipment and discussed critiques of their training exercises by an outside observer. Based on this self-assessment, the officers

found several opportunities to improve the service they provide in fire water system walk-downs and specific improvements they could make in communication during a fire fighting situation.

Root Cause Analysis

In some cases, an organization finds that the same issues keep surfacing year after year. Every time there is a planning meeting, the same gaps are identified. There may even be a history of failed attempts to close a particular gap, so that no one is even willing to work on it any longer.

In this case, the root cause analysis process can be very effective in opening up new possibilities for understanding the nature of the gap that exists.

Figure 6.10.   Elements of Effective Root Cause Analysis

1. Identify area or issue for analysis.
2. Select method of analysis.
   - Five whys
   - Barrier analysis
   - Process diagrams
   - Change analysis
   - Risk tree assessment
3. Perform the analysis.
4. Change the system to fix the root cause.

While there are a variety of root cause analysis methodologies, most were created to investigate major accidents. As I mentioned in Chapter 2, the method that often lends itself to the strategic planning process is the technique known as the Five Whys. In this method, the question "why?" is asked at least five times until the root cause of the problem is understood. Then, new actions that will address the root cause can be planned.

> Example: A laboratory had a recurring problem with technicians who would not wear their safety glasses. Training had been conducted and safety posters and signs clearly indicated the need for safety glasses. A root cause analysis used the five-why questioning method. Why did the technicians not wear their glasses? Because they worked with research scientists who often did not wear their glasses. Why did the research scientists not wear their safety glasses? Because they thought it was not important and a bother. Why did the laboratory management not enforce the requirement with the research scientists? Because they did not want to upset the brilliant scientists.

There are other approaches to root cause analysis that can be effective in closing gaps in a strategic plan. Barrier analysis, for instance, can be used to investigate a quality problem once it has occurred, but it can also be useful in anticipating what might go wrong with a process or system and providing barriers to help avoid the potential failure.

> Example: An organization experienced problems with corrosion in a 500,000-gallon chemical storage and treatment tank and determined that this was a critical long-term strategic issue. A team was organized that included representatives from the organiza-

Figure 6.11. Barrier Analysis

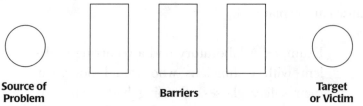

| Source of Problem | Barriers | Target or Victim |

- Identify the source of a failure and the target or impact of the failure.

- Identify the barriers that should protect the target.

- Assess the effectiveness of each barrier.

- Add new barriers as needed.

tion's engineering, operations, development, and maintenance groups, and was facilitated by the author. The storage and treatment tank was being used in a state-of-the-art chemical treatment process. A barrier analysis was conducted to identify what barriers were actually in place, and what needed to be in place, to ensure that future problems would not occur. The analysis revealed deficiencies in design, operations, and inspection that were then addressed by the line organization. While the design and operation where theoretically sound, recommended developmental studies were unfunded, so unanticipated corrosion was not found by a laboratory design study. An adequate inspection program had likewise not been funded.

Statistical Process Control

In some cases, the gap to be closed can best be addressed by applying statistical tools and concepts to the situation. There are a variety of statistical tools for analyzing data that will enable organizations to better understand the causes of poor performance, scrap, rework, and customer dissatisfaction.

Figure 6.12.   Elements of Effective Use of Statistical Process Control

- Employ a qualified statistician in establishing the statistical process control program.
- Educate the workforce to collect and interpret the data.
- Distinguish between common cause and special cause variation.
- Distinguish between statistical control limits and manufacturing tolerances.

Certainly the broader management concepts taught by Deming can be applied in a wide range of areas, even where the more immediate use of tools such as control charts may not fit. Deming's admonition to avoid numerical goals, for instance, is sound advice for any kind of strategic planning venture. Setting a specific goal often automatically limits the amount of progress you will achieve.

> Example: A plastics manufacturing firm was experiencing scrap rates as high as 40 percent in preparing molded plastic parts for their customers. The company relied on multiple inspectors to catch the bad parts. Solving the high scrap rate and reducing material and inspection costs became a major strategic objective for the company. The company hired a statistician to consult with them on establishing attributes and variables control charts to help create an understanding of the variation in their systems. Consistent use of statistical data allowed the organization to pinpoint the sources of their scrap problems and to greatly reduce their costs.

Through the use of control charts and Pareto diagrams, the statistician helped the employees recognize the sources of variation that were causing the plastic parts to fall outside the customer's specifications. In many cases, bad parts were being produced early in the process and not identified as scrap until far down the production line, after they were painted and heat treated.

Establish Strategic Partnerships

In some cases, the best enabling action for achieving a strategic objective is to establish a strategic partnership with another organization. Cooperation with another organization can provide a win-win opportunity for both organizations to achieve their objectives without having to add resources.

A manufacturing organization can reduce the number of vendors by partnering with a specific supplier that meets its quality criteria, controls costs, and provides just-in-time delivery of materials. A school can partner with a business to obtain adjunct instructors. City governments can partner with businesses to obtain executives on loan for specific projects. A hospital can partner with a nursing or medical school to make it easier to recruit new personnel. A voluntary organization can partner with other voluntary organizations on specific projects of mutual interest.

Example: The state vocational school system in Kentucky decided to implement a total quality management process as a key strategy for the 1990s. Rather than hiring a consulting firm to train the school managers across the state, each region identified local industries that had successful TQM processes in place and obtained free training and facilitators from these companies. Local companies have been pleased to participate in this partnership because improved vocational education means an improved pool of people from which to recruit.

Use the Right Tool to Get the Job Done

Organizations can really suffer when people get locked into ideological battles about which tools to use and which guru to follow. Some people, for instance, place no value at all on the traditional quality tools, such as design review and auditing, and want to focus only on project teams. Others deem the whole effort as futile unless the quality effort is built around statistical tools. The objective of the quality professional is not to uphold a particular dogma or to peddle an exclusive set of tools. The objective should be to assist an organization in accomplishing its mission by applying the resources of the quality discipline and selecting the best tools to help get the job done.

In some cases this may mean the use of small project teams to go after inefficiency and waste. In other cases, it may mean taking a big broom to the system, such as organizational redesign or reengineering, and making a clean sweep. In still other cases, the organization may have effective systems in place but need audits and peer reviews appropriate to the work being performed.

Figure 6.13. Application of Quality Methods

Control existing systems	Improve existing systems	Create a new system
• Design and peer review	• Project teams	• Process redesign
• Auditing	• Cycle time reduction	• Root cause analysis
• Inspection	• Statistical process control	
• Statistical process control		

It is the quality manager's responsibility to advise the planning team and the line managers about the tools available within the quality discipline and to help them choose wisely which tools will help identify and close the gaps.

All of the tools mentioned in this chapter can be used in a variety of circumstances. The purpose here is not to teach these tools, but to show their use within the context of strategic planning.

Once the best tools are selected it is time to get on with their implementation and measure the progress.

Chapter 7

Implementing and Tracking Results

Once an organization has identified the objectives it needs to achieve and the actions it needs to take to close the gaps between the current state of the organization and the desired future state, it is time to get down to the business of implementing plans and tracking the results. The quality manager must help the organization develop a system for tracking the performance of the planned actions.

The issue of measuring improvements in quality raises numerous questions and difficulties. Should the organization focus on measuring the implementation of the action plans, or should it focus on the objectives in the strategic plan? What, exactly, should be measured? How should implementation schedules be made? Who owns the implementation of quality plans and who should be held accountable? These are tough questions. Regardless of how they are answered, the organization must define and use specific action items to achieve the mission and vision, and the effectiveness of these must be tracked.

The key point about measuring the progress of the strategic plan implementation is that both the objectives and the enabling actions need to be tracked to provide the fullest perspective of progress.

Figure 7.1.   The Strategic Plan

MISSION
and
VISION

The strategic plan

has specific action items:

• Expand statistical process control training

• Improve customer satisfaction survey system

• Audit quality records

• Introduce more teams

Progress in implementing the strategic plan needs to be tracked and managed.

Measuring Processes and Results

There is a lot of debate among managers, quality profession-als, and consultants over what and how to measure as organi-zations implement quality improvements. Some argue for focusing on bottom-line results while others want to focus the measurements on the processes that are producing the results. Measuring both the process and the bottom line often turns out to be the best course of action.

Measuring the implementation of enabling processes certainly makes sense. Benchmarking, for example, may be an action your organization has decided to take to improve quality. It is not your product. Measuring the amount of benchmarking that is going on will give you some useful feedback regarding your progress in implementing your improvement plan. If zero benchmarking visits have occurred this year, you know that there will be zero new ideas flowing into the organization.

Measuring the level of an activity provides feedback on whether the activity is happening, but it still tells you nothing about the results of the activity. We may see data that indicates ten benchmarking trips have occurred, but this does not tell us if the benchmarking improved our processes. The level of activity could appear to be very high, but the results could still be zero, if people are not following up on the ideas gained from benchmarking. This is the primary criticism of measuring the rate of activity of the enabling quality strategies alone. The measure may indicate a great deal of action that signifies little.

Figure 7.2.

	Measure the processes	Measure the bottom line
Pros	• Allows for tracking of the enabling actions. • Aids in diagnosing implementation problems.	• Focuses on results. • Gets people excited.
Cons	• Shows activity, not results.	• Does not shed any light on the cause of good or poor results.

If performance measures focus on the bottom line, they reveal the consequences of the activities that have been initiated in the organization. For example, an organization may decide to track the amount of scrap being generated in a production line. It will be easy to develop a graph that gives visible feedback to track and trend the information. Suppose the bottom-line indicator of scrap level just hovers at the same level, month after month. The indicator tells you that no improvement is being made, but does not offer any clue as to why. To find that out, you will need to look at an indicator for some enabling quality strategy, such as whether or not those benchmarking trips are being made, that will help redesign the work processes.

The combination of process and bottom-line indicators offers information on both the cause and the effect occurring within the organization. By combining both process and bottom-line indicators, the quality manager and others can obtain the best perspective of the real situation in the organization. If the bottom line shows no progress, but the indicators show lots of action, then examine the process for activity traps.

Figure 7.3.   Optimum Indicators for the Strategic Plan

Measure the process	and	the bottom line
• Number of teams working to streamline processes	and	Overall output or costs
• Cost savings from individual projects	and	Bottom-line costs
• Number of employee suggestions to solve customer problems	and	Number of customer complaints

This approach can be well illustrated by the quality measurement process employed at Xerox. In-process measures are designed for each of the elements of Xerox's strategic plan, and are correlated with bottom-line results.[1] A rating system exists to evaluate each element in the plan for the effectiveness of its approach, its deployment, and its results. While the Xerox strategic plan covers a five-year period, an annual management assessment evaluates the in-process measures

---

1. Richard C. Palermo, ed. *A World of Quality: Business Transformation at Xerox* (Burr Ridge, IL: Business One Irwin, 1993), 120.

and the bottom-line results to determine what changes should be made.

Learning from the Baldrige Award

A great deal of thought and experience went into the establishment of the seven categories for the Malcolm Baldrige National Quality Award. The award criteria represent a well-balanced view of the issues that influence organizational performance, so they can be extremely useful in planning how to evaluate the implementation of a strategic plan.

In most cases it will be advantageous to develop at least one evaluation criterion to give feedback on each of the seven award categories. Using these criteria does not mean that an organization should focus on winning a Baldrige Award. Instead, it allows the organization to assess the quality performance of an organization. In particular, it allows organizations to examine perspectives of their quality implementation that they might not have been eager to discuss otherwise.

Figure 7.4. The Baldridge Criteria Can Help Any Organization Achieve Excellence

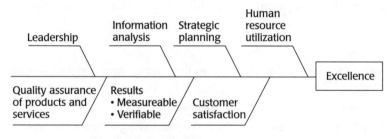

Even before an organization starts to set up performance measures to track the strategic plan, the award criteria can be used to evaluate the plan itself. Are all seven

categories addressed in the plan? Does the plan over-emphasize or underemphasize specific aspects of the Baldrige system?

As a tool to assess the strategic plan, the Baldrige criteria can be very valuable. However, care should be taken not to allow the scoring system in the criteria automatically to influence the emphasis in the organization's strategic plan. An organization may have the greatest need for strengthening an area that is not one of the higher numbered areas. The organization should meet its own needs, first of all. Also, be aware that the relative values of the Baldrige categories are open to a considerable amount of debate, depending upon one's orientation to the quality profession.

The quality manager needs to decide how to advocate the use of the Baldrige criteria—or any other standard—to the other senior-level managers in order for the concept to be well received. The use of an external standard can be presented as valuable for comparison. Managers might have concern about using an external standard if they perceive the objective is to go after an award, or if it means spending time answering survey questions or dealing with outside auditors for no clear benefit. An external standard can be well received if it is pitched as a quick way to make use of already established knowledge.

Figure 7.5. Use a Standard Such as the Baldrige Award to Assess Your Strategic Plan

Baldrige criteria	Our plan
1. Customer satisfaction	1. Our plan has major focus in this area and specific action items.
2. Human resource utilization	2. Our plan has actions to develop cross-functional teams and self-managed teams.
3. Leadership	3. Our plan just assumed leadership– need to revisit this and work on this issue.

Let's take a look at how each of the seven Baldrige categories can be used to identify enabling actions to support an organization's strategic objectives.

Customer Satisfaction

It will be valuable to identify one or two measures that allow an organization to determine how well customers' input is integrated into the various organizational processes. This means, for example, developing an indicator to determine whether the organization has an adequate customer satisfaction measurement system in place. A hospital can measure whether a customer satisfaction process is used in every organizational unit, for instance. It can mean having an indicator that tracks whether or not customers' needs and ideas are included in the organization's planning processes. For example, a bank can measure the extent to which customers of each branch office are asked for feedback about services. A volunteer agency can track whether or not the agency's customers are taken into consideration when activities are planned. The presence or absence of customer involvement can be measured for each of the agency's subgroups and functions as attributes data. A city government can measure whether residents are consulted prior to decisions that will impact communities and services. A data sheet can be created to show the extent of citizen input into decision making.

These are measures of enabling actions that will give some feedback on whether the organization is on the right track in pursuing its quality objectives. When the answer indicates that the clients, customers, or citizens are not being consulted, then there is a need and opportunity for improvement. But without the indicator, how would anyone know? We would just assume that we are pleasing the customer since we talk about pleasing the customers.

Do not be fooled into measuring actions that provide no benefit to achieving the strategic objectives. Do not count the number of quality posters on the wall. The gap between what is said and what is done can make this type of data very misleading.

Figure 7.6. Example of Actions Based on Customer Satisfaction Goals

Goals	Actions
Consult customers regarding plans.	a. Form a focus group to ask customers if they are being consulted and for ideas for improvement.
	b. Make sure that customer survey forms are sent out on schedule.
	c. Assess managers on how they use and respond to customer surveys.

Human Resource Development and Management

The Human Resource Development and Management section of the Baldrige criteria offers several possible approaches for measuring the rate of implementation of quality in an organization. Organizations can measure the number of special project teams or the number of people who work in empowered teams, with either a facilitator as leader or as a self-directed team.

In large organizations it is important to keep the percentage of employees working in an empowered manner in mind, rather than just the number of people or the number of teams. It can, for instance, sound very impressive to see that there are two hundred empowered teams in an organization, or that there are one thousand employees working in empowered teams. However, if the total population of the organization is twenty thousand people, then having a thousand people in empowered teams means that 95 percent of the workforce is not working in an empowered structure.

Figure 7.7. Example of Actions Based on Human Resource Criteria

Goals	Actions
Involve employees in local quality improvement efforts.	a. Check to make sure everyone is trained in improvement methods.
	b. Remind managers to encourage involvement.
	c. Audit several local group meetings and encourage people to participate.
	d. Include questions about participation in next work force survey.

Human resources consists of numerous systems that can be flow diagrammed and measured. Cycle time for these systems can be determined and non-value-adding steps can be eliminated. Rework can be identified. Root cause analysis of employee complaints, labor disputes, and litigation can be conducted to improve the systems.

In assessing the degree of focus on human resources development and management in the strategic plan, the quality manager—or members of the planning team—can look for actions related to streamlining the recruitment and hiring process, employee satisfaction with the benefits program, and the use of data in controlling absenteeism.

Unfortunately, the human resources professionals in the organization may also have to face the fact that many of the cherished practices in the field of performance feedback and compensation have been hurting their organization's ability to sustain a commitment to quality and mission success. It is the quality manager's role to point out the areas where human resources practices are a barrier to achieving quality performance, and work with that department to develop new systems to better meet the organization's needs.

The most common problem areas involve compensation and performance appraisals. If an organization seeks to organize around a team approach, then human resources will need to modify its compensation package so that a larger part of each person's compensation is determined by team performance. Likewise, when performance is affected by variation in systems, as Deming often argued, the system for appraising employee performance needs to be reexamined so that employees are not penalized for problems beyond their control.

> Example: A tire company was penalizing employees who produced bad tires by forcing them to stay over after their shift and continue to make tires until they had made up for the scrap tires each had produced during the day. When control charts were introduced, it soon became evident that the variation in the production machines' capabilities guaranteed that scrap tires would be produced regardless of how diligent the employee might be. It was impossible to make 100 percent perfect tires on the existing equipment. The human resources practice had to change.

Sometimes in developing a strategic plan, the planning team focuses on external customers, improving equipment, and closing the gaps using a variety of quality tools. The human resources systems are often overlooked. Using the Baldrige criteria for assessment will help ensure that the important HR issues are not overlooked by the team or by the organization.

Management of Process Quality

By assessing the strategic plan with the Baldrige criteria, the planning team will consider whether they have adequately addressed the need to improve their organization's processes.

The criteria suggest that an organization should examine its management of process quality, and there are numerous ways to accomplish this. One approach is to measure the number of improvement projects in process and the number of improvements that have been implemented. If there are many ongoing projects to improve the product design process, the service delivery process, or the measurement system, the organization is making progress on the management of process quality.

This area should have a bottom-line indicator in addition to quantifying the enabling processes. A final indicator that shows customer satisfaction levels, scrap rates, or the amount of rework in a process shows whether improvement is being made in process quality.

The bottom-line indicator of success in a chemical production plant is the number of production cells on stream producing product within specifications. Preventive maintenance and maintenance repairs to bring equipment back on line are the critical processes that are evaluated in the factory since they determine the availability of cells on stream. The plant has a bottom-line indicator (cells on stream) and a process indicator (time required to perform maintenance work) that can both be measured. Management focuses its attention on projects that shorten the maintenance cycle time, thereby improving the bottom-line indicator. Specific projects may deal with finding new methods to perform in-situ repairs on operating cells or improved preventive maintenance that lengthens the operability of a production cell. Shortening the cycle time required to perform a maintenance task has a direct impact on the bottom-line indicator of cells on stream. The strategic plan will call for optimizing the output of the existing production cells. Enabling actions will center around continuous improvement of the maintenance function that will be achieved through specific projects. The success of each project can be measured and related both to the bottom-line indicator and the strategic plan.

Figure 7.8.   Example of Actions Based on Management of Process Quality Goals

Goals	Actions
Improve delivery of materials to customers.	a. Interview the customers to identify their needs. b. Flow diagram the delivery process. c. Study process for delays or unnecessary work. d. Conduct brainstorming exercise with employees to improve the system.

In the business sector, evaluation of the effectiveness of managing process quality is readily linked to strategic objectives, such as profitability and customer satisfaction. For example, consider the case of Blue Cross–Blue Shield of Ohio. Their strategic measures are costs, number of members, and a ranking by the National Management Information System (NMIS). By focusing on process quality, they were able to reduce costs by $40 million in one year, acquire 130,000 new members, and move from second-to-last place out of 73 providers up to fourth place in NMIS ranking. They accomplished these feats by maintaining a strong focus on process quality—improving customer claims processing, examining the patterns of customer calls, shortening claims turnaround time, and achieving 99 percent accuracy on customer claims.[2]

The planning team should ensure that the organization's processes are being analyzed in order to maximize the value of quality as a core value in the organization.

---

2. Sheila J. Smith, "Blue Cross–Blue Shield of Ohio: A Profile in Change," *Quality Progress* vol. 28, number 10 (October 1995).

Leadership

Developing a performance indicator to measure quality leadership is one of the most difficult challenges of the Baldrige criteria. Wallace Company, the 1990 winner of the Baldrige Award, defines leadership as a core part of its commitment to quality:

> We know that leadership is an essential element for our company's success. At Wallace Company, Inc. leadership means working closely with all associates, endorsing pride of workmanship, listening to and responding to the suggestions of those closest to the job, building in quality in all aspects of operations, focusing performance on the positive, and developing a team spirit. (Wallace Company Mission Statement).

Everyone would agree that effective leadership is the cornerstone for an effective strategic plan. The question is, what is it, and how do you measure it?

There are several approaches for describing effective leadership. At a minimum, the leader should be strong in creating an empowering work setting, effective in involving people in setting goals, able to establish an expectation that performance measures and quality tools are used, and proactive in establishing an environment of teamwork. Other assessments of leadership might add other attributes, but these four are the core.

One of the best approaches for assessing quality leadership in an organization is for the quality manager or an organizational development specialist to survey people in an organization regarding their impressions about how management leads. This can be accomplished by either conducting a specific survey of employees regarding their view of management's leadership, incorporating questions about quality leadership into an existing periodic survey, or incorporating quality leadership as a factor in a 360-degree performance review system. Many organizations conduct employee surveys on some established time sequence. By including questions that allow employees to express their opinions regarding management's leadership, management can gain valuable feedback regarding whether or not their quality-centered strategy is actually understood and embraced by the workforce.

The new advances in 360-degree performance feedback can also bring leadership issues to the surface. Ann Ewen is one of the pioneers in designing and implementing 360-degree appraisals. Ewen has found that the use of 360-degree appraisals allows the organization to assess not only the typical quantitative results (i.e., what was accomplished), but how it was accomplished as well.[3] Leadership behaviors as well as the behaviors of team members such as cooperation, planning, and delegation skills, can be assessed.

Assessment tools can be used by the quality manager to audit the degree to which managers in the organization are providing the type of leadership required to achieve the objectives of the strategic plan. An effective instrument will provide feedback based on responses to survey questionnaires given to the manager's employees, peers, and higher management. Kouzes and Posner's leadership inventory survey, "The Leadership Challenge," gives managers feedback from a variety of perspectives, such as the extent to which the manager

---

3. Ann J. Ewen, "Enhancing Performance Appraisals with 360-Degree Feedback: Impacts on Users' Perceptions of Fairness." *Proceedings of the 23rd Annual National Energy and Environmental Symposium,* American Society for Quality Control (1996), 78–85.

challenges employees to set high goals and stretch in order to grow personally and improve the organization. Stephen Covey's evaluation survey from the *Seven Habits of Highly Effective People* workshop offers insights into how an individual communicates and behaves that have a great impact on what the individual is able to accomplish. There are many other assessment tools that can provide managers feedback about their leadership styles. For example, XICOM's "Power Base Inventory," developed by Kenneth W. Thomas and Gail Fann Thomas, provides feedback regarding how a manager uses information, personal knowledge, the goodwill of team members, positional authority, rewards, and discipline to obtain organizational goals.

Most existing leadership surveys are rather broad in scope and not designed directly around a theme of quality-centered management. However, these types of feedback surveys can easily be employed to provide the leaders with feedback about how their behavior influences the organization and can be very useful in improving quality-centered management, even when it is not specifically called out in the instrument's language.

While these surveys may be useful, some organizations will prefer to design their own survey focusing on the leadership behaviors they believe will directly impact quality. An organization may wish to structure its survey to address specific areas that relate to internally driven or externally driven behaviors. For instance, the organization may have based its quality program on an ISO standard, or on Baldrige criteria. Specific behaviors that support the standard or award criteria can be identified and included in the survey. Internally driven criteria may result from behaviors that the chief executive identifies as supportive of the organization's mission and vision. At Lockheed Martin, for example, senior management has identified leadership attributes that include empowerment, goal setting, the establishment of quantifiable goals, and leadership through team-building. These would be the natural attributes to focus on in designing a leadership assessment instrument for that organization.

On pages 151 through 153 is an example of a survey that was designed to help an organization assess the leadership styles of managers and supervisors in a manufacturing setting based on total quality management attributes identified by Norm Augustine of Lockheed Martin. The survey instrument was designed in two parts. A TQM leadership assessment survey form is given to employees by a facilitator. Each employee completes the questionnaire for his or her manager, supervisor, or team facilitator. The results from the employees in the crew, group, or team are tallied by the person who administers the survey, keeping the individuals' input anonymous. Results are transferred to the TQM leadership profile, which is then given to the manager of the employees who completed the survey. The quality manager, or a staff member, meets with the line manager and provides the feedback, and can discuss what actions can be taken to improve the scores.

This form can be customized for a specific factory, hospital, government agency, or service organization.

If leadership is an important aspect of a successful strategic plan, then an organization needs to take some time to assess how well leadership is performing in this area. In addition to the individual feedback, it is important to survey the organization to determine how well the quality message is delivered and received. A feedback survey that can be divided by organizational units is very helpful for determining the size of the gap between an organization's rhetoric about quality and the actual behaviors and beliefs of people in the organization.

TQM Leadership Assessment Survey

Instructions

This survey is designed to assess the actions or activities your supervisor or team leader demonstrates in support of total quality management. For each of the 20 statements, circle the response that best describes your supervisor's behavior.

Do not sign this evaluation page.

EMPOWERMENT	Never	Seldom	Some-times	Often	Always
1. Maintains or builds the self-esteem of people in the group	1	2	3	4	5
2. Keeps people in the group informed about what is going on	1	2	3	4	5
3. Leads team meetings in a way so that everyone participates	1	2	3	4	5
4. Encourages people to make decisions and plan their own work	1	2	3	4	5
5. Provides visibility and recognition to group members	1	2	3	4	5

GOAL SETTING	Never	Seldom	Some-times	Often	Always
1. Involves everyone when establishing group performance goals	1	2	3	4	5
2. Encourages the group to continually make improvements in how work is done	1	2	3	4	5
3. Encourages people to take time for effective planning	1	2	3	4	5
4. Keeps the group focused on its goals throughout the year	1	2	3	4	5
5. Encourages the group to benchmark excellent performance by other groups or companies	1	2	3	4	5

QUANTIFICATION	Never	Seldom	Some-times	Often	Always
1. Involves the group in establishing quantifiable performance measures	1	2	3	4	5
2. Encourages people to use statistical tools to measure performance	1	2	3	4	5
3. Displays performance measures prominently for all to see	1	2	3	4	5
4. Informs the group about budget and financial information	1	2	3	4	5
5. Encourages group members to obtain training in the use of statistical tools, problem-solving, and TQM methods	1	2	3	4	5

TEAMBUILDING	Never	Seldom	Some-times	Often	Always
1. Encourages team members to cooperate with each other	1	2	3	4	5
2. Encourages cooperation with customers and suppliers	1	2	3	4	5
3. Encourages the team to jointly develop plans, make decisions, and solve problems	1	2	3	4	5
4. Demonstrates effective listening skills	1	2	3	4	5
5. Creates an environment of trust and enthusiasm	1	2	3	4	5

When you have completed this survey, give it to the survey administrator. Your supervisor will receive a statistical summary of all the data but will not see the survey form you completed.

TQM Leadership Profile

The people in your work group each completed a survey regarding your leadership and support related to total quality management. There were 20 behaviors assessed. For each behavior the evaluation scale is:

5 = Always   4 = Often   3 = Sometimes   2 = Seldom   1 = Never

[The cumulative mean is the mean score for everyone surveyed to date.] Your feedback for the 20 behaviors is:

EMPOWERMENT	Mean Score	High Score	Low Score	Cumulative Mean
1. Maintains or builds the self-esteem of people in the group	_____	_____	_____	_____
2. Keeps people in the group informed about what is going on	_____	_____	_____	_____
3. Leads team meetings in a way so that everyone participates	_____	_____	_____	_____
4. Encourages people to make decisions and plan their own work	_____	_____	_____	_____
5. Provides visibility and recognition to group members	_____	_____	_____	_____
TOTAL EMPOWERMENT SCORE	_____			

GOAL SETTING	Mean Score	High Score	Low Score	Cumulative Mean
1. Involves everyone when establishing group performance goals	_____	_____	_____	_____
2. Encourages the group to continually make improvements in how work is done	_____	_____	_____	_____
3. Encourages people to take time for effective planning	_____	_____	_____	_____
4. Keeps the group focused on its goals throughout the year	_____	_____	_____	_____
5. Encourages the group to benchmark excellent performance by other groups or companies	_____	_____	_____	_____
TOTAL GOAL SETTING SCORE	_____			

QUANTIFICATION	Mean Score	High Score	Low Score	Cumulative Mean
1. Involves the group in establishing quantifiable performance measures	_____	_____	_____	_____
2. Encourages people to use statistical tools to measure performance	_____	_____	_____	_____
3. Displays performance measures prominently for all to see	_____	_____	_____	_____
4. Informs the group about budget and financial information	_____	_____	_____	_____
5. Encourages group members to obtain training in the use of statistical tools, problem-solving, and TQM methods	_____	_____	_____	_____
TOTAL QUANTIFICATION SCORE	_____			

TEAMBUILDING	Mean Score	High Score	Low Score	Cumulative Mean
1. Encourages team members to cooperate with each other	_____	_____	_____	_____
2. Encourages cooperation with customers and suppliers	_____	_____	_____	_____
3. Encourages the team to jointly develop plans, make decisions, and solve problems	_____	_____	_____	_____
4. Demonstrates effective listening skills	_____	_____	_____	_____
5. Creates an environment of trust and enthusiasm	_____	_____	_____	_____
TOTAL TEAMBUILDING SCORE	_____			

Those organizations that want to use surveys to assess the employees' perceptions about management's leadership should remember that it is not necessary to survey everyone. A representative sample gives excellent data at lower costs, even if it is not as emotionally satisfying to everyone in the organization who wants the opportunity to be heard.

Figure 7.9. Examples of Actions Based on Leadership Goals

Goals	Actions
Improve leadership of quality effort.	a. Provide advanced quality training to a critical few managers.
	b. Conduct an assessment survey and give managers feedback.
	c. Survey employees for ideas on how the organization can improve.

Information and Analysis

Another way to audit the content of the strategic plan is to review the organization's plans in the area called Information and Analysis in the Baldrige criteria. Quality information refers to the data that is collected that describes the performance of systems. Quality information can include information generated through audit reports, control charts, peer reviews, design reviews, and any other tool. It is important to assess whether the organization is collecting the information it needs and how it analyzes the data it collects.

There are a variety of ways to measure the implementation of processes related to quality information and analysis. One approach is to examine whether people are trained to handle quality information, such as statistical data, process measurements, and test and laboratory data. People need to be educated to understand the importance of accuracy, precision, and variation in data, along with the need for protecting the honesty and integrity of data. Another method is to measure whether the analysis of data is being performed properly. Are people using the right calculations? Is the data being recorded in a manner so that it can be retrieved?

It stands to reason that if people are not trained to handle quality information and to analyze data, then they will not be doing so in the workplace. Training is an enabling activity, not an end in itself. So, measuring the volume and content of training tells if people are prepared for working in a quality-focused arena, not whether they are actually utilizing the skills and concepts they have been taught.

An organization can measure the percentage of people who have completed training in the quality disciplines, such as the use of statistical tools, courses on problem solving, or teamwork. The absence of this type of training is a reliable indicator that the actual use of the tools is not occurring out in the organization.

The presence of a healthy amount of training, however, does not, in and of itself, ensure that the knowledge is being applied. People in an organization need to know what to do and need to be encouraged to do it. For this reason, it is useful to measure the number of processes that use control charts or to count the number of times that a formal problem analysis method is utilized. It is important to measure whether each workplace in the organization has its own performance indicators posted in a place where all employees can see the feedback from their efforts.

Figure 7.10. Example of Actions Based on Information and Analysis Goals

Goals	Actions
Ensure that people are trained in and using quality tools.	a. Check training records.
	b. Form focus groups to ask people to identify areas where they need more training and the barriers to using tools.
	c. Form a team to attack barriers.
	d. Conduct an audit for use of quality tools.
	e. Review focus group and barrier attack, and audit feedback at mid-year management meeting off-site.

Strategic Planning

How does an organization go about auditing its effectiveness in strategic planning?

The most effective measure will be a form of attributes data—go or no go. Either there is a strategic plan or there is not. Either quality is in the mission statement, or it is not. Quality is either reflected in the vision or values of an organization, or it is not. Either there are strategic objectives related to quality in the organization's plan, or there are not.

Another measure of the strategic planning process will be the frequency by which the plan is reviewed; this is covered in the next chapter. A plan that is developed and then set on a shelf to gather dust is of little value. How does the organization keep the plan alive?

Still another approach to measuring the effectiveness of the strategic plan is to measure the amount of benchmarking done. Benchmarking often indicates the degree to which an organization is actively seeking to improve. Low benchmarking suggests low interest in improvement. High benchmarking suggests an intense drive for achieving higher quality. Of course, the act of benchmarking alone may only be an activity trap if undertaken by the wrong people, or if outside perspectives are devalued by influential people within the organization.

Quality and Operational Results

There are a myriad of possible performance measures to provide feedback as to whether an organization is studying its quality and operational results. The presence of bottom-line indicators, such as scrap rates, customer complaints, cycle time improvement, and, of course, the bottom-line operational costs, are important criteria. When organizations are not paying attention to these indicators, there is a problem with the strategic plan.

The question is not whether to assess the bottom-line quality and operational results, but how to do so from a perspective that supports quality. It is in this arena that Deming offered some of his strongest rebukes regarding the management of many American companies. The focus on the bottom line, according to Deming, must be a focus on the long-term bottom line, not this quarter's or this year's numbers alone.

The key implementation issue regarding quality and operational results is to ensure that the review of results takes the long-range perspective about the organization, not the short-term approach. Focusing on short-term results to guide the organization is by its very nature not a strategic approach to quality.

Creating Action Plans

Regardless of whether or not your organization chooses to use the Baldrige criteria for evaluating the implementation of a strategic plan, you will need an action plan that defines *how* to close each gap that has been identified.

Figure 7.11.   Action Plans

What	Why	How
A document that defines the actions to be taken, the person(s) responsible, and time frame for completion.	To define roles and responsibilities and provide a tool for tracking implementation.	• Define actions. • Gain commitments. • Agree on deadlines.

An action plan defines what action will be taken, who is responsible for getting it accomplished, and when the action should be complete. While this sounds simple, it can be surprisingly complicated. There should be an action plan item for every gap identified in the strategic plan.

For example, the voluntary organization that was building homes identified the need for volunteers to supervise home construction if an accelerated level of building was to be achieved. This was identified as one of the more difficult and important steps in their strategic plan. It needs an action plan to ensure that it is accomplished.

Who is responsible for recruiting volunteers? A specific member of the organization must be tasked with the responsibility of recruiting the construction supervisors. When are they needed? They need to be identified and in place by the middle of spring so they can be ready to pitch in when construction picks up.

In most cases, identifying who will do what by when is an excellent action planning process. In some cases, with the most critical items in a plan, it is valuable to take some time and assess what problems might occur in a plan and why. With the source of potential failures in mind, it is possible to improve the plan by adding actions that will prevent it from failing. For example, recruiting the construction supervisors might fail if it is not clear what their roles and responsibilities will be. Prospective volunteers might shy away if they are given vague descriptions of the roles and responsibilities of a construction supervisor's duties. Preparing a job description can head off this possible problem.

Figure 7.12.   Steps in Developing Effective Action Plans

1. Actions are identified based on the strategic planning team's work.
2. For each specific action, identify who will be responsible for getting it done.
3. Discuss and agree on completion deadlines with each person responsible for completing an action.
4. Put the whole plan in writing, showing actions, responsible people, and deadlines.
5. Ask yourself, "What can go wrong with this action plan?"
6. Build in additional steps or actions to keep the things that can go wrong from derailing the plan.

Unfortunately, in planning to improve quality, just as in planning for anything else, we often assume that because we are doing it, everything is going to go just fine. Other people's plans may fail, but ours will be okay. Whether the plan is to implement statistical process control or to form empowered work teams, there needs to be a healthy amount of probing for what might go wrong with the plan, not to back away from following through on the plan, but to identify the potential weak spots and to improve the plan so that the weak spots can be buttressed.

It is the quality manager's role to provide this questioning. He or she must ensure that action plans are developed with commitment for implementation from the line organization.

Gantt Charts

The Gantt chart is a valuable tool for planning and tracking progress of action plans developed in the strategic plan. The tool is named after its creator, one of the fathers of the school of scientific management, Henry Gantt, who created a scheduling chart which allows people to track the implementation of a plan over time.

The typical Gantt chart identifies a goal to be accomplished and breaks it into steps that will be accomplished over time. For instance, a Gantt chart can be employed to help an organization institute a quality auditing program in a retail store. The steps in the plan would include the identification of areas to audit, the training of auditors, the development of an auditing schedule, and the notification to store managers of the purpose for the auditing process. With a Gantt chart, the steps would be broken out along a time line to help visualize how the work will be accomplished.

By breaking down the steps and displaying the information along a time line, it will be easier to assess whether the appropriate steps are being done on schedule. The chart will

Figure 7.13. Example of a Gantt Chart For Implementing a Quality Audit Program

Goal	October	November	January	February
Identify areas to audit.	X			
Train auditors.		X	X	
Develop an audit schedule.			X	
Notify store managers.				X

be familiar to planners in the manufacturing arena, but people conducting strategic planning in the government, retail, or volunteer sectors may find it a new and useful tool.

Ownership and Accountability

Ideally, everyone who is a player in the strategic planning process will be enthusiastic and ready to support the actions required to achieve a higher level of quality. This is not always the case, and even when everyone is a willing supporter, there are often other commitments in life that keep people from following through on all that they need to do.

For this reason, it is vital to establish ownership and accountability for all of the enabling actions that will close the gap between where the organization is today and where it wants to go. Whether through the creation of action plans or the use of a tool such as the Gantt chart, the planning team must create an outline defining what will be done, when, and by whom.

Juran's admonition about quality improvement is extremely important when it comes to implementing the strategic plan. Improvements in quality happen only when people get organized to make them happen, as Juran noted. They do not occur simply because we are well-intentioned people. Improvement occurs project by project, and in no other way—meaning that each improvement, each closing of a gap to achieve an objective, must be treated as a project to be planned, organized, and carried out.

Without action plans and Gantt charts, the strategic plan will not provide the organization with the results that are needed for success. When people invest their ideas, concerns, hope, and energy in developing a plan, they must see a tough and thorough commitment from their leaders to follow through with the most important issues that have been raised. When people are permitted to not address problems, when it is perceived as okay to have a low commitment to achieving the actions in the plan, then people lose faith in the planning process, the vision, and the organization itself. The Gantt chart gives the organization a tool for visibly tracking the progress of multiple plans, thereby providing a meaningful tool for establishing and maintaining accountability.

Chapter 8

Reassessing and Reenergizing the Plan

"On no other stage are the scenes shifted with
a swiftness so like magic as on the great stage
of history when once the hour strikes."
Edward Bellamy, Looking Backward (1888)

You have defined your strategic objectives and identified the gaps between the current state and the desired future state. Action plans to close the gaps are in place and people are now moving to implement the action plans. Gantt charts are used to assess the progress. The energy level is high, and people are enthusiastic about implementing the changes they have helped plan.

Then new issues crop up that grab everyone's attention. The competition does something exciting. A new election focuses people on different issues. New technology appears that will make all of your plans obsolete. A new competitor enters the market and threatens your market share. Some people in your organization are still trying to implement the plan, but others are drifting in other directions. Before long, people have forgotten what the plan was all about.

What went wrong? Nothing! That's just the way things happen in organizations. Organizations are like spinning tops. You pump them up with new energy and they spin for a while. After a while, they start to lose their energy and begin to wobble. The trick is to pump in some more energy before all your efforts fall apart.

Organizations obey the rules of the universe, especially the principle of entropy. Entropy describes the process by which a system will lose energy and become more disorganized over time. In the beginning of the strategic planning process there is a great deal of enthusiasm and focus. Over time, the system loses energy, enthusiasm wanes, people lose their focus on the strategic objectives and gaps that need to be filled. Members of the strategic planning team will be excited in forming the plan, but in implementing it over time, the energy will dissipate. Issuing a written plan helps to keep the energy level up.

At some point, the plan will become obsolete and probably forgotten by most of the people who were involved in developing it. Before this happens, the quality manager should establish a process to reassess the plan and to develop new strategies for the organization. If the plan is allowed to go completely fallow, then the organization will be adrift, so it is vital to take steps to renew the plan in order to keep the organization focused.

Strategic planning is a cyclical process, as pointed out in Chapter 1. The quality manager needs to reiterate this point with the senior-level management over time. Line managers who fail to grasp this reality will complain about having to begin the process anew, so the quality manager must keep reminding the line management of the need for a cyclical planning process.

The Shewhart Cycle

The Shewhart cycle, advanced by Deming, can give us insight into the cyclic nature of planning. This model suggests that organizational transformation requires a repeated process of assessing the need for change, planning change, implementing the change, and checking to see that the changes have been effective.

Figure 8.1.   The Shewhart Cycle

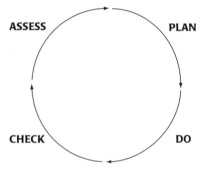

Most planning processes are gung-ho on the assessment phase, where we identify the gaps between where we are and where we want to be. The change process occurs when people start implementing their action plans, and the observation phase occurs as people use indicators to determine whether or not the desired changes are occurring. But, what about the final phase, the study of results, which leads to a new round of assessment?

Both Shewhart and Deming were insightful in their advocacy of a change process that is cyclic, rather than linear. We get organized with a lot of energy to make change happen, go forth and start implementing the change, and then stagger back in, exhausted and distracted by other events. Then, after a spell, we are ready to start again. So, it is natural for the plan to run out of steam over time, and for people to take a step or two back, and to assess how far they have come and where they now need to go.

Who Needs to Assess the Progress?

At this stage in the process, some line managers can have a tendency to close ranks and allow only a few people to be involved in assessing how well the strategic plan is being implemented. This type of information can be regarded as very sensitive, because people are afraid of failure, and fear has not been driven out of the organization. Organizations that tend to have strong centralized management hierarchies may be reluctant to share information that indicates how well the organization is progressing. However, it is important for the strategic planning team to have access to the information on the progress being made in closing the gaps.

Sharing the ongoing performance information with the entire planning team may seem tedious and time consuming. To be efficient, managers often rationalize a justification for leaving the team out of the assessment phase. The more entrenched an organization is with a hierarchical management system, the more likely that the planning team will be nudged out of the information loop over time.

The quality manager plays the primary role in preventing this potential problem. Keeping the planning team up to date on reports and active in meetings where implementation status is discussed becomes an important role for the quality manager.

The team that worked together to develop the strategic plan needs to gather periodically to assess the plan. To exclude people who developed the plan from its evaluation will strip them of their ownership and send them a message that the organization does not value them enough to share information and seek their opinions.

It was noted in Chapter 1 that the strategic planning team should consist of a diagonal cross-section of the organization in order to ensure that all of the key perspectives are included in developing the plan. Ensuring diverse perspectives improves the content of the plan and enhances the reception of the plan's content throughout the organization.

The same rationale applies to the evaluation of progress toward achieving the objectives and closing the gaps. If the only people who are reviewing the progress all hold one point of view or perspective, for instance that of upper management, they can be fooled by the information they see. For example, if nurses are left out of the process of evaluating a hospital's quality efforts, then administrators may make a judgment about patient care that misses their unique understanding.

Assessing

The assessment of the implementation of the strategic plan must answer two basic questions:

1. Are we on track toward achieving our goals?
2. Are our goals still the right ones?

Figure 8.2. The Strategic Planning Team's Role in Assessing Implementation of the Plan

1. Review action plans and Gantt charts.
2. Determine whether the organization is on target to achieve the goals.
3. Keep asking if the goals are still the right ones.

Set the stage for the assessment step by first collecting the data that provides evidence on how the organization is progressing toward achieving the objectives and enabling actions. Then, begin by asking the team to decide if the organization's vision is still the same as when the planning process began, or whether the vision needs to change and the organization needs to set a new course. If there is a need to redefine the vision, jump right into doing it on the spot. Don't spend time studying data about past performance that may no longer be important. Deming used to call that activity driving by looking in the rearview mirror. Hang on to the data, however, since it may be useful at some future time.

If the vision has remained constant, then compare the current condition of the organization with the desired future in the vision. Have you closed all the gaps? Which ones remain open? Plan what additional steps may be needed to do a better job of closing the gaps.

You also need to ask if the environment in which the organization works has changed, creating new gaps between the current state and the desired future state. If new gaps have emerged, then develop objectives to close the gaps, design enabling actions, and put actions in place that will fix the new problems.

In most cases, the assessment process can be brief. If there is consensus that the organization is moving ahead in the right direction, then the assessment process needs to focus only on clarifying the next steps and celebrating the successes.

In other cases, which require more time, the assessment reveals that the implementation of the plan has gone astray, but that the goals are still valid for the organization. This situation will require some examination of how the plans got off track, as well as formulation of new plans.

In a few cases, the implementation goes well, but the goals need to be changed in order to accommodate such conditions as new budget restraints, new technology, new international competition, or a new face in top management. However, the organization can address these challenges knowing it has already proved its ability to implement change.

Figure 8.3. Assessment of the Progress Made

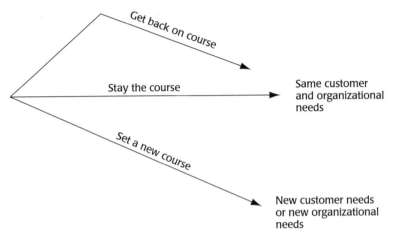

Assessment of the Progress Made in the Strategic Plan Can Lead to Several Options

Get back on course

Stay the course → Same customer and organizational needs

Set a new course

New customer needs or new organizational needs

If the organization does need to set a new course, it is vitally important to recognize the people who helped implement the goals in the plan, even as the plan is being changed. If the quality manager allows good contributors to go unrecognized because their accomplishments are overshadowed by events, then people in the organization will become reluctant to invest their energy in achieving the new goals for fear that their efforts will be neglected when the goals change again in the future.

The most challenging situation is when the implementation goes poorly *and* the basic goals shift due to changes in the organization's situation. Such a case may require starting from scratch.

Staying the Course

When an organization assesses its plan and finds it is making good progress toward objectives that are still valid, then the challenge is to stay the course. This means the quality manager must keep people throughout the organization excited about the journey that remains. It's important also to celebrate the success that has been achieved thus far.

To stay the course, it is necessary to identify the action items that remain unfinished. These action items should be assessed to determine if they will still work, and there should be a renewal of resources to ensure that the final steps are carried out on time.

For instance, an organization may have decided that an important gap to remedy was training in the use of control charts. Training was held and half of the work force is now trained. Where to go from here? The need still exists. Renewed energy should be directed to getting everyone trained, making sure that control charts are actually in use, and ensuring that the training is having the desired effect.

The difficulty with staying the course is that management must look toward the long term and take actions for the long-range benefit of the organization. If management is thrown off course by every little breeze that blows across the bow, the organization will soon be steering in circles.

Changing Directions

Sometimes there is a need to change the direction of the strategic plan. In most cases, this means that the recognized gaps still need to be closed, but new issues have arisen that are also going to require actions in order to close new gaps between where the organization now is and where it needs to be.

The quality manager helps prepare people for the possibility of changing directions by two activities in the strategic planning process. First, when the planning team generates their force field analysis, they are envisioning possible sources of change that could impact the organization. This process helps the team conceive of the future as rich with alternatives and subject to influence by events. Second, by establishing scenarios with each implementation plan, the team reinforces the perspective that future conditions are subject to change and that plans can be made to respond in a manner that still supports the established goals.

> Example: Five years into a successful quality improvement effort that used project teams to improve process quality, a chemical plant was confronted with a new national health standard that required more protective clothing for workers, extensive use of respirators, and sitewide monitoring. The plant was able to apply its teamwork approach to the challenge by reallocating staff resources and charging the project teams to find the best methods for meeting the new challenge.

Figure 8.4. Factors to Consider in Making Mid-course Changes to the Strategic Plan

1. Involve the original strategic planning team in the decision to make mid-course changes.
2. Determine which actions in the plan need to be continued and decide how to keep up momentum in those areas.
3. Give new objectives the same level of planning as those the original plan (i.e., force field analysis, action plans, Gantt charts).
4. Set the new course and continue to assess.

In another example, an organization has identified the need to involve people in decision making and is halfway through its plan to create empowered work teams. However, there is a new mandate to reduce costs, so the organization wants to focus on reducing scrap. A new action plan must be developed to remove the causes of poor quality that lead to scrap. It will damage the organization to halt the previous efforts to create empowered teams. To do so would send the work force a message that management was not really serious about involving people in decision making. A better approach is to build the new action plan on the successes that have already occurred. Working with the strategic planning team, the quality manager, in collaboration with human resources and line management, involves the empowered teams in the new effort to root out the causes of scrap. Of course, individual efforts by employees who are not on teams must be encouraged and recognized, too. However, if the rush to meet a new objective, such as reducing scrap, causes management to weaken their support for earlier objectives, the employees will soon become cynical and consider the whole quality effort to be just a fad.

Celebration

There are many opportunities to celebrate success in organizations. Sometimes we celebrate the extra effort of an individual or a team in performing a task. Sometimes we celebrate when an operational unit reaches some particular milestone.

In some cases, celebration appears to be a random act by management. Good efforts that contribute to strategic objectives go unnoticed, while special attention is given to people for doing things that don't strengthen the strategic position of the organization. This presents a real problem.

There should be specific times and events which are regularly planned and designated for recognizing success. Part of the planning for recognition should involve the review of the strategic plan to determine where people have been successful in taking actions to support the plan.

It helps to establish a team to oversee the celebration process in an organization. The team can establish guidelines and standards for recognition and can review candidates and make decisions regarding which people or teams should be recognized. Using a team, which represents a cross-section of the organization, provides an effective method for ensuring that the recognition process remains balanced throughout the organization. The team approach will give the recognition and celebration process consistency and attention so that celebrations are not neglected in the daily rush of events.

> Example: At a Lockheed-Martin manufacturing plant, the company and its two unions, Oil Chemical and Atomic Workers and United Plant Guard Workers of America, jointly conduct an awards and recognition program. A joint union and management team reviews nominations for recognition and hosts a Crew of the Month program to celebrate the efforts of crews in improving safety, enhancing quality, reducing cycle time, reducing scrap, improving customer satisfaction, and reducing costs.

If your organization includes employees who are represented by a bargaining unit, it is vital to involve official representatives of that unit to help in the planning and administration of the celebration process. Bargaining units have specific concerns about how people are rewarded that need to be respected in order to have a successful celebration process.

Rededication

An organization's initial strategic plan needs to be shared with all the stakeholders in the organization. The identity of the stakeholders depends on the type of organization, but normally includes employees, investors, and clients. Having a strategic plan that is only accessible to an elite few renders the plan next to worthless.

The strategic plan can be condensed and published for all employees as a pamphlet. It can be documented by a videotape that shows the viewer specific examples of enabling actions and features customers and their opinions. The plan can be printed in sections in an internal newspaper, or put on e-mail for employees to access. The more emphasis given to the plan, the greater the likelihood of employee support of the plan, if it was developed in a participative process.

It is the quality manager's role to ensure that the contents of the plan are communicated to the workforce. The method may require cooperation from senior-level management and different groups within the organization. However, the quality manager is responsible for communicating the plan.

Figure 8.5. Example of an Effective Celebration of Strategy

Strategic Goals	Actions	Celebration
Improve overall contact with customers.	a. Survey customers. b. Streamline the advertisement development process. c. Use customer survey input to modify advertisements. d. Put customer feedback forms in the new ads.	Host a Friday pizza lunch for the advertising department and give everyone the afternoon off.

Likewise, when the plan is reassessed and updated, the modified version of the plan needs to be shared with everyone. People need to know where their organization is going in the long run, if they are to be expected to support the organization's objectives. Sharing the perspective of the strategic plan allows everyone in the organization to identify the ways in which they can contribute to the success of the plan. Issuing the revised plan gives them a sense that change is occurring, and that they are key players in the change process. For example, Motorola has an effective process for communicating their key quality strategies to all employees using face-to-face interaction, publications, videoconferencing, e-mail, and videotapes. Texas Instruments' Defense Systems and Electronics Group has a communication approach that allows all their interlocking teams to stay current with their quality strategy. Ritz-Carlton Hotel has transformed their old "Daily Line-Up" meetings into a tool to emphasize the company's quality program. Weekly and quarterly communication meetings at Zytec are the cornerstone for discussing all of the details of their quality strategy.[1]

Be sure that the introduction of the plan is done in a manner which is consistent with the organization's goals. If the organization is placing an emphasis on being environmentally friendly, or is focused on reducing costs, do not send out an expensive multicolor publication. Send out something on recycled paper printed with one color. If the organization's plan is communicated in a way that contradicts the organization's values, it will become an object of ridicule.

Dealing with Skeptics and Cynics

Every organization has its fair share of skeptics and cynics who will receive the revised strategic plan with question and abuse. Skeptics will doubt that the organization can achieve the goals that have been set. While they accept the concept of strategic planning, skeptics will question the content of the

---

1. Laura Rubach and Brad Stratton, "Mixing Mediums Is the Message" *Quality Progress* vol. 28, number 6 (June 1995).

plan. They may question management's commitment to closing the gaps that have been identified. To win over the skeptics, the revised plan needs to be shared along with the acknowledgment of past successes and failures. The successes need to be rewarded and the failures admitted, along with a statement of the lessons learned from the failures.

Cynics doubt both the process of planning and the content of the plan. Cynics have given up on the organization's ability to work effectively, and discount any efforts to change as futile. The quality manager will need to recall that being a cynic is a learned behavior. It can be unlearned by sustained evidence that the planning process is really participative, by inviting people to join in, by acknowledging the lessons learned from failure, and by a commitment to improve in the future.

> Example: A group of campus chaplains was assembled by their denomination to conduct a strategic plan for ministry at seven universities in the mid-South. Although the ministers were cordial with one another, their enthusiasm for developing "another plan" seemed rather low. Each of these men and women was accustomed to working on their own campus, and their experiences with efforts for centralized planning had left them skeptical that anything positive could result from another such endeavor. In this case, however, the chaplains were challenged to create a unified vision of what a successful ministry would entail, using their own experiences and dreams. They had the freedom to acknowledge past failures and successes. Rather than having to respond to someone

else's plan, they created their own vision, which raised the energy level of the group. They quickly agreed on four broad objectives that would enable them to achieve their vision. Each chaplain then developed specific enabling actions relevant to his or her own campus, and they all agreed on specific actions the pastors in their area could also take that would support the work of the campus ministries. The mood changed dramatically from "here we go again" to a strong sense of ownership when the participants were actually given control of the strategic planning process and the freedom to express their real opinions.

Chapter 9

Overcoming Obstacles to Strategic Planning

"Mere talk about quality accomplishes little."
W. Edwards Deming

Talking about quality does not provide results. Results occur only when people get organized to improve their work processes, as Juran noted. A haphazard effort at strategic planning will be seen as a fad within any organization, unconnected to the organization's real business objectives. The strategic planning process connects all of the components of the quality program, steering the organization in a sustained campaign to achieve high quality, thereby satisfying its customers and creating its future.

Some organizations have managed to make tremendous gains in the quality arena, gains that are real and can stand up to the scrutiny of evaluation by a neutral board of examiners. Most organizations, however, have been only partially successful, because they do not have a real strategy on which to build their actions.

Why is it that some organizations are unable to develop a strategic focus on quality? Why do some organizations envision the future as something that cannot be influenced or should not be thought about? Why do many leaders fail to see the connection between quality and the success of their organization? What can be done within organizations to change this situation?

There are at least four barriers that keep organizations from starting down the strategic planning path. These barriers are woven into the culture and belief system of organizations that cannot take proactive steps to influence their own future. They are:

- An inward focus, which precludes any examination of world-class business practices.
- Limited understanding and interpretation of quality.
- A pattern of leadership that creates a docile and unenthusiastic work force.
- An obsession with current problems that never seems to end.

Figure 9.1. Barriers to Strategic Planning

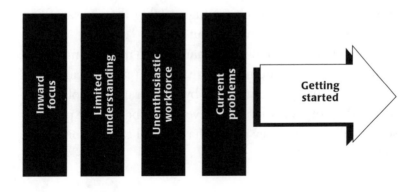

Focusing Inward

If an organization's managers focus inward, they will never look outside to contemplate what customers need. An inward focus ascribes to the belief that if things are not broken, they should not be fixed. There is an unspoken belief that next year will be just like this year, and since we are okay this year, why worry about next year?

While most organizational models depict managers at the top of the hierarchy, it might be more accurate to envision the managers in the center of a sphere. The sphere's outer shell consists of people who have direct contact with customers. An inwardly focused management remains content to work on issues within the sphere.

Internal focus in a school system could be managers looking at test scores and ignoring parents' concerns. In local government, it could mean looking at activities accomplished instead of citizens' opinions. In a factory, it could mean lack of attention to or concern for the customers' satisfaction.

> Example: A company won a government contract to install new equipment at a federal facility. The contractor had a strong internal focus on being 100 percent error-free, meaning that nothing would leave their shop to be installed until it was perfect. This value had served them well in other settings; in this case, however, the customer's emphasis was on meeting a schedule. The customer diverted work in order to create a time window for the equipment to be installed. Bugs could have been eliminated once it was in place. The date arrived for the installation and the vendor did not show up. The vendor's internal focus on

perfection cost them all their future contracts
with that specific agency.

Customers' perspectives rarely permeate into the
inward-focused organization in most cases. The problem
with the inward focus is that it generates a contentment with
the status quo that leads to a resistance to change. Many
organizations refuse to implement any form of strategic planning because things are going well, which is precisely the
time that an organization can make the best use of the
process. They wait, instead, until a crisis is upon them and it
is almost too late to take meaningful action.

Using Benchmarking

What can be done to challenge the inward focus? Benchmarking is the best approach to getting people to look outside
their organization to see how others are succeeding. Unfortunately, benchmarking often becomes an active tool in organizations only when things are in really bad shape. When the
organization is in severe trouble, the leadership will wake up
to the situation and start to benchmark, or be replaced by
new leadership that has an awareness of practices outside of
the organization.

It is the quality manager's role to insist on an organized
approach to benchmarking for the organization. If a quality
manager determines that the organization is suffering from
an inward focus, then the manager must find data about the
competition or market trend information that will encourage
the organization to look outside its boundaries in developing
a strategic plan.

An effective benchmarking program will begin by examining the gaps that were identified in the strategic planning
process. The quality manager then checks with his or her peers,
or consults a database, and determines what organizations have

already proven excellence in the area that his or her organization needs to improve. Once permission to benchmark is obtained, a benchmarking team is assembled that creates a list of questions and performs a site visit. After making first-hand observations, the benchmarking team assesses what they saw and decides how to implement these ideas back in their own organization.

However, in the case of dealing with an organization with an inward focus that presents an obstacle to strategic planning, the strategic plan may not exist, or it may be ineffective, ending up on the shelf gathering dust. In this case, the quality manager wants to identify a company that has a reputation for successful quality-centered planning and bottom-line results that will capture the attention of the senior management team. The quality manager then challenges the senior management team to benchmark the other organization, knowing that the managers will observe a vibrant, quality-centered strategic plan when they make their benchmarking visit.

Benchmarking can either be a tool used late in the game, or a tool used proactively by a management that is dedicated to staying ahead of the pack by engaging in continuous learning.

Use an Outside Guru

When an organization's senior-level leaders resist looking outside of their organization, the change intervention must focus on these senior-level people, such as the city's mayor, the plant's manager, the company's president, the hospital's administrator, the school district's superintendent, or the college's president.

The key intervention strategy, in this situation, is to arrange for the senior person to have contact with the right, highly credible person who can properly impress on the senior manager the need for a strategic approach to quality. The senior person must have the opportunity to make this discovery for himself, and come back to the organization and announce this new revelation.

For example, a successful manager of a research and production organization believed that the company's existing quality program, which focused on inspection and control, was adequate. He felt that the company did not need an aggressive continuous improvement campaign. The quality manager for the organization could not personally convince the senior manager of the need for a quality strategy that included continuous improvement. So, the quality manager arranged an opportunity for the senior manager to attend a one-day briefing with Dr. Joseph Juran. After that briefing, the senior manager was a champion of quality improvement as a core principle for the organization.

Each person involved in implementing quality practices has experienced a moment when the light bulb clicked on about quality. This experience must be honored in other people when it occurs, and their new discovery must be treated with respect. If you are the quality manager for your organization, there are many basic realizations you have about quality that most other people do not have. Part of your job is to arrange for other people to discover for themselves the things that you already know.

Sometimes people learn about the importance of quality by reading about it. Some people are persuaded by factual evidence of the benefits, some people learn about quality by listening to their peers. Some learn best by sitting with a guru who can provide personal guidance and perspective.

The best approach to take in helping people learn about the need for quality is to try all approaches. While there are tools that can help predict a person's learning style, the odds are low in most organizations that the quality manager will have access to that type of information. So, plan a blitz campaign, using articles from magazines and speakers from local organizations that have successfully integrated quality into their business strategy. Schedule your senior-level people to attend a meeting where they can hear the message directly from a guru. If this is outside of the organization's budget, look for a video conference sponsored by a local community college or a program sponsored by your Chamber of Commerce.

Figure 9.2.   The Problems and Solutions Flow

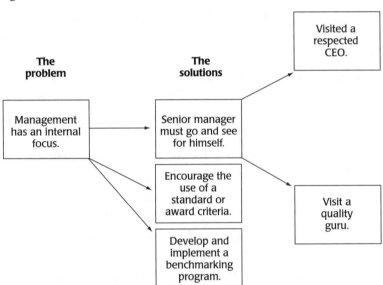

There are two sources of inspiration that senior managers may respect enough to listen to regarding quality. One source is the senior managers from other companies who have built their success on a quality-oriented strategy. The other source is the handful of very experienced quality gurus. The quality manager must make arrangements for the senior-level manager to attend a seminar held exclusively for senior managers that will feature either a highly qualified quality guru or a very successful senior manager.

If this approach works, the quality staff needs to be prepared to accept the fact that the manager will have discovered quality on his or her own and will tell you everything you already know as if it is brand new. Do not expect to be recognized for having labored many years on selling or implementing these ideas. It just does not work that way.

Use a Standard or Award Criteria

Using an objective evaluation tool or standard is a third approach to changing an organization's inward focus. Many organizations find that comparing themselves to a standard is an effective way to highlight both the strengths and weaknesses of their quality efforts. There are international standards, national standards, and standards for specific industries.

The quality manager has to make a judgment call in selecting the type of standard to advocate. An international standard such as ISO 9000 and a national standard such as the Baldrige Award both offer effective quality strategies. An industry-specific standard might have more appeal in some cases, such as the NQA-1 standard for organizations in the nuclear industry and ISO 14000 for organizations whose operations may impact the environment.

However, if an organization has an inward focus, why would it want to compare itself to a standard? If things are going okay, why will the managers want to subject themselves to information that would challenge their comfort with their current situation?

The quality manager needs to find the right "buttons" to push with his or her management in this case. The buttons will be different for each organization. In many cases, man-

Figure 9.3. Strategic Benefits of Standards and Awards

Standard or Award	Benefits
ISO 9000 series	• Meets customer-mandated requirements to be considered a viable supplier. • Process-oriented focus on improving the quality of systems will reduce costs and enhance competitive position.
ISO 14000 series	• Assures viability as a supplier with a reputation for responsible environmental quality management. • Protects the organization's image. • Minimizes risk of costly problems and fines.
Industry-specific standards such as NQA-1, military specifications, or medical standards.	• Assures full compliance to challenging regulatory requirements. • Minimizes total life-cycle costs of major projects. • Maximizes assurance of public safety.
Baldrige Award Criteria	• Maximizes probability of out-performing competition and achieving global market dominance. • Elevates quality to become the driving force and aligns the entire organization with a quality-centered focus.

agement's interest can be gained by focusing on how this type of evaluation can identify areas to examine for reducing costs. It might help to bring up some customer concerns or other problems that can be addressed through the use of a standard.

In many cases, the effective use of a standard only comes after the quality manager has already convinced the senior-level manager to address quality as a key organizational strategy. The standard is then used as a tool to broadly open the door to expose the organization to world-class performance expectations.

Limited Understanding and Interpretation of Quality

There is a broad range of perspectives on how to understand and achieve quality. The best strategic planning process occurs in organizations that subscribe to a broad quality definition and integrate those principles into every activity.

When people perceive quality only as a reactive conformance to requirements, then quality ceases to be a meaningful factor in the organization's vision. Conformance to requirements is important but is not a complete embodiment of the quality discipline. A broad definition of quality as a proactive philosophy and set of tools makes strategic planning possible. If the organization's vision of quality is simply not to make mistakes, then there will be no employment of quality as a driving force in the organization.

Figure 9.4.   Hierarchy of Perceptions of Quality

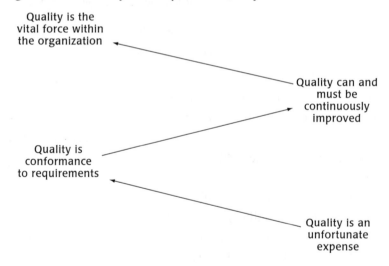

What should be done if the organization's historical understanding of quality is based upon a belief that quality is conformance to requirements? As in the case of the inward-focused organization, this situation calls for a specific learning process in order to gain a new and broader understanding of quality.

How can you help your organization perceive the multiple facets of quality? Introduce the Baldrige criteria as an assessment challenge. Acknowledge the important role of conformance to requirements within the criteria, but point out the other proactive aspects of an overall quality effort.

Another action is to identify an organization, similar to your own, that has a broader application of quality; you can point to it as an example of how quality can be better understood. Encourage people to try to benchmark this organization's quality initiative to discover how quality is practiced in a more strategic manner. It is always advisable for the quality manager to create an opportunity for people to discover new insights about quality. In order to use either the Baldrige criteria or another organization as a model, the quality manager must stay current with the literature of the quality profession. Access to periodicals such as *Quality Progress, Quality Digest,* and the *National Productivity Review* are vital for identifying good sources to employ as examples.

A Pattern of Endullment

An effective participative strategic planning process will not occur in a culture of "endullment," the dulling of people's minds as a result of their nonparticipation. Nonparticipation leads to low motivation, poor attendance, refusal to cooperate to improve the system, and learned apathy.

The concept of endullment originated in the field of education through the work of Ira Shor at Columbia University. Shor found that classrooms that do not involve students will ultimately "endull" them. When students have no choice regarding what to learn or how to learn, they are turned off by learning. This initial disinterest in learning eventually leads to passive resistance, such as playing hooky, not doing homework, or just not responding to questions in class. Active resistance can be addressed through discipline and expulsion, so students often learn to resist passively.

Figure 9.5. The Pattern of Endullment

	Symptoms	Causes	Solutions
At school	• Don't do homework • Skip school • Complain	• No student input to curriculum • Teacher controls everything	Involve students in designing their learning program
At work	• Don't do work • Call in sick • Complain	• No worker input to decision making • Boss controls everything	Involve workers in making decisions and controlling the workplace

This concept of endullment also applies in the workplace. When people are not involved in decision making in their work, they become endulled over time. When people have little or no input into or understanding of the strategic direction of the organization and how their work makes a difference, they will be turned off by working. Just as in the classroom, this initial disinterest in the organization also leads to passive resistance, such as calling in sick, incompletely performing work, and not offering ideas for improving the workplace.

Once an organization begins to develop a pattern of endullment, it can easily slip into reification. Endulled people resist the strategic planning process because they deny their own ability to influence the future. A culture of endullment treats scrap and rework as a normal part of the job. The concept of continuous improvement will never take root and grow among endulled workers and managers.

Overcoming endullment, whether in the educational system or the work environment, can happen only when leaders make a concentrated effort to change their style of leadership. Managers must change their leadership style

Figure 9.6.   Endullment Traps People

from controlling to facilitating. The leader-facilitator engages the workforce in participating in the work process, challenging them to take ownership and responsibility for improvement. Middle management must encourage and support the front-line facilitators when they strive to involve their staff.

An organization that is strongly controlled from the top can definitely produce a strategic plan, and it may be a very good plan. However, the plan will be limited by the blinders that the top managers have on. Vital information may be filtered out by middle managers. The best strategic plan will be developed by a team that includes people from all levels of the organization. To encourage this type of involvement, management needs to see itself as conducting the energy of the organization, not as controlling what everyone in the organization is doing.

The Sisyphus Syndrome: An Addiction to Crisis Management

Sisyphus was the legendary figure in Greek mythology who was doomed to spend eternity rolling a large stone up a hill.

At night the stone would roll down, and the next day he would repeat the process.

The Sisyphus syndrome describes those organizations that fixate on dealing with the crisis of the moment. An issue that is not really a crisis, is seized upon as a crisis. Management, along with most of the employees, spends the day rolling that stone up the hill and goes home with a sense of accomplishment. The next day, there are similar stones to be moved. This goes on and on, creating an environment in which the strategic issues are never addressed.

In some cases, organizations really do not have any crises to deal with. Routine activities that add little value to the organization become the stones. Whether they are legitimate crises or activity traps that steal the energy of the organization, they contribute to a facade of purposefulness within the organization. People believe they are doing well because they can see all that is getting done, regardless of whether they are really working on important issues.

Figure 9.7. The Crisis Culture

In a culture of crisis, managers achieve a sense of immediate accomplishment. Crisis spurs action, deadlines, meetings, and excitement, all of which create the impression of progress.

This activity can become addictive and can lead people to avoid both short-term and strategic planning. For Sisyphus managers, nothing seems to be happening when people are planning. They would rather stop this planning nonsense and get out there and solve the problem of the day. The persistent lack of planning for quality ensures that there will be a steady supply of rocks ready to be rolled.

The Sisyphus syndrome presents an ideal opportunity for utilizing the services of an outside consultant. It is usually advantageous to use an outside consultant rather than an internal person because this problem will require a human sacrifice of sorts. To solve the Sisyphus dilemma, someone must confront the organization's dysfunctional behavior, which is usually the behavior spawned collectively due to one or two people at the top. No internal person can provide this confrontation and expect to survive. Therefore, an outside consultant should come in; give an objective, "expert" diagnosis; deliver the bad news; and then leave.

The downside of using an outside consultant is that some outside consultants do not know how to work effectively with their clients. Some consultants see themselves as the knight on a charger who has arrived to save the organization. Usually, the quality manager knows what needs to be done or said. The consultant's role is to give the message validity, or to perform a specific part of a change process.

A skilled outside quality consultant can give the bad news to the "guilty" people in a quiet manner that saves them from embarrassment. If the bad news comes from an internal source, the diagnosis will probably be discounted and the messenger will be doomed.

An experienced consultant will understand the role that he or she needs to play in this situation. They know they must play many roles, and sometimes it is their job to help a client by carrying the bad news that is too dangerous for anyone in the organization to deliver.

Using a Standard to Confront Crisis Management

An impartial quality standard can be employed as another approach to dealing with the Sisyphus syndrome. A standard, such as the Baldrige criteria or a Baldrige-based state award, can be used as a contrast to the behaviors that perpetuate crisis management.

To use this approach, the quality manager needs to create an opportunity for the organization's leaders to reflect on their behaviors. This can be done by conducting a senior management workshop. In the workshop, a facilitator instructs the participants to work in groups to assess the organization's performance compared to the selected standard. In this way, the managers discover for themselves where they are trapped in activities and focused on crises, and where they need to redirect their attention to develop a long-term strategy for achieving high quality and success for the organization.

Using a seminar setting for this process of discovery has several advantages. First, when the Sisyphus syndrome is discovered by the people who suffer from it, they have an "ah-ha!" experience that can motivate them to change. When other people, like the quality manager, try to tell managers that they have this problem, then the afflicted people will respond with denial. Second, the therapy for curing the Sisyphus syndrome requires a group effort. By confronting the problem as a group, the managers can begin to create their process for developing a strategic plan, which is the only long-term recovery for crisis addicts.

Chapter 10

Blitz-Building
Your Strategic Plan

"Be ready on time."
Shoichiro Irimajiri
Honda of America

Perhaps you have looked over this book and decided to invest your time and energy in developing a strategic plan for your organization. Or, as a quality manager, you are now convinced that your organization needs a strategic plan in order to consolidate initiatives and give it focus. The important question becomes: How do I get moving with this process, and how long will it take?

As a rule of thumb, implementing an organization's strategic plan takes about as long as it takes to build a house. A small organization's plan, like a small house, can go up rather quickly. Big organizations, like big houses, take longer. The good news, however, is that with some planning and facilitation, the actual building process can go pretty fast.

In addition to teaching and facilitating in the quality field, I serve as president of one of the first local affiliates of

Habitat For Humanity. Years ago, Habitat learned that there are two ways to build a house. One approach is to plan and build at a steady pace over many months, as time, money, and volunteers are available. This is an effective strategy that has provided many people with good homes.

A second approach is to carefully plan the layout of the house, and line up the materials and volunteers so the construction work can all be completed in one day. This is called blitz-building a house. The advantage of the blitz-build is that it gives a sense of accomplishment to the participants and provides a dramatic change in a neighborhood. One day there is an empty lot, perhaps with a slab of foundation, and the next day there is a house, with a family ready to move in. Both approaches require careful planning and expert construction supervision, but the blitz-build requires flawless planning and supervision.

You can build your organization's strategic plan along either of these construction models. The plan can be worked on a piece at a time over many months, in a low-key manner, so that a product gradually emerges without much apparent investment of resources. Or, after some careful preparation, you can assemble the right team and blitz-build the plan in just a day or two.

In today's fast-paced organizational climate, there are many advantages to going with the blitz-build model. It not only gives the planning team a tremendous sense of accomplishment, but gives the quality manager a dramatic and tangible product.

When you blitz-build a house with a hundred volunteers, you still have to follow all the right steps and be able to meet all the housing codes. There must be a foundation, plumbing, framing, insulation, roofing, and finishing. Likewise, when you blitz-build a strategic plan, you must consider your customers' needs and how you will meet those needs; know your organization's values and the forces that will influence your future; and develop objectives, scenarios, and plans to close the gaps. With the blitz-build, you just do it all really fast.

Behind-the-Scenes Planning

In a blitz-build, there has to be some behind-the-scenes planning. This is done by the quality manager, with input from line management and the help of the facilitator who will lead the actual planning session.

Guidelines for Blitz-Building The Strategic Plan

1. Prepare
   A. Review existing mission, vision, and values statements; strategic plan; and quality plans and salvage what you can.
   B. Select your planning team.
   C. Pre-work for the team:
      1. Review documents
      2. Conduct focus groups
      3. Benchmark
      4. Attend conferences
2. Practice
   A. Ensure good location and food.
   B. Ensure the tools are ready.
   C. Check out each planning step and determine how it will be implemented.
   D. Mentally walk through the actual planning session.
3. Do it!
   A. Build the strategic plan.
   B. Celebrate.
4. Follow-up
   A. Document.
   B. Publicize.

C. Track it.

D. Renew the effort.

1. Prepare

First, take a look at the organization's existing mission statement, vision, values statement, or strategic plan, to the extent that these exist. What can you keep and what do you need to discard? Is there an existing plan that can be utilized?

If there are some good building blocks for your new foundation, it is to your advantage to keep them, since it saves time and money, builds a sense of continuity with the past, reinforces good ideas that the organization has already invested in, and avoids offending the people who worked on these earlier efforts. However, if there is no mission, vision, or values statement, you will have to create them as an opening step in the planning process. This can be done quickly, if you use a facilitator.

After reviewing the existing documents for useful building materials, work on identifying your planning team (see Chapter 1) and ensure that your team has the right mix of people to be effective. While the mix is important to provide a diverse perspective, it is also essential that the individuals selected be regarded as reliable within the organization and that their opinions are trusted and respected.

To get your team ready, involve them in some pre-work, that is, assignments they will complete prior to the planning session. Pre-work can involve a review of the existing mission, vision, and values statements, asking each person to edit and draft their own ideas about these documents.

You can involve the team members in focus groups with customers and employees (see Chapter 2) to provide them with the broadest possible perspective of what the plan needs to address.

Benchmarking is another effective form of pre-work. Formal benchmarking, with site visits, is an involved process, but it may be possible to get this information via media and/or industry associations. Or, send the planning team to an appropriate quality conference where they can sample a wide range of success stories in just a day or two.

Information can also be obtained through a literature review. There are many journals that focus on sharing success stories. A follow-up phone conversation with the subject or author of a journal article can be as valuable as a benchmarking trip.

2. Practice

It helps to verbally walk through the agenda for the "building" phase of the planning process in order to work out any potential problems.

First, consider the location; always go to some neutral territory. Get out of the plant, out of the headquarters, off the campus, away from city hall—maybe even go out of town. My personal experience suggests that you find out what the team would prefer, within reason, and take them there.

Next, consider food. You have to feed your blitz-builders, and they will get hungry fast. Also, make sure there will be beverages and convenient restrooms. I once witnessed a meeting of high-level managers totally break down due to a lack of cookies, so be sure to feed your participants. Or, as one sage facilitator taught me, "They can't all talk at once when they've got their mouths full." For some groups, this will mean providing lots of food!

Then, look at the tools you will need to support the group process. This usually means flip charts, easels, tape, and markers, but it could include a telephone capable of conference calls or a laptop computer. (You might want to add hand puppets that the participants can use for voicing the opinions that no one wants to be quoted as having said. (If I can use hand puppets with high-ranking military officers— admiral and general rank—you can use them anywhere.)

It is necessary to walk through the building process before you assemble the team at the off-site location in order to make sure you will not be trying to put the roof on first. So, check out each strategic planning step in this book and see that you have a method to make it happen. Here are some examples:

1. Use pre-work focus groups to ensure that your team members begin with the customer in mind (see Chapter 2).
2. Be ready to refine or create a mission statement that has quality as a core concept (see Chapter 3).
3. Be ready to prepare or adjust the vision and values statements (see Chapter 4).
4. Use a time line exercise (Chapters 2 and 5) to build a common perspective within the team.
5. Use a force field analysis (Chapter 5) to assess forces that will impact the organization.
6. Clarify the key objectives and discuss scenarios (Chapter 5).
7. Develop plans to close the gaps between where you are now and where you want to be (Chapter 6), drawing from all the quality tools.
8. Agree on action plans (Chapter 7).

Check out the agenda several times and ask: "What can go wrong?" Refine the agenda and keep asking probing questions until you are comfortable that the planning session will flow smoothly and be effective. List things that might go wrong, and focus on the items that have a high probability of happening and will have a serious negative consequence if they do happen. Then, take some actions to prevent these from occurring.

The facilitator needs to be able to visualize how the actual session will work, with all the parts fitting together. When the facilitator can visualize the flow of the entire session, he or she is ready and the chances are very good that the meeting will be a success.

The toughest thing to plan is "soak time." Ideas need time to soak in; people need time to reflect, wrestle with ideas, and abandon old notions. It is best to plan breaks and meals for soak time. But be prepared to push the group onward before too long.

3. Do it!

Then get your team together and spend a day or two creating the strategic plan.

The facilitator's role is to push the process and stay out of the content. The participants should address the content of the plan. The quality manager needs to be free to influence the content and should mentally shift gears every now and then to make sure the process is on track. The quality manager should not try to facilitate the process. As the most senior manager who is devoted full-time to the organization's quality concern, the quality manager must be free to focus almost all of his or her attention on the content of the session.

Be sure to close the session with some celebration, in whatever manner is appropriate to the norms of your organization. In some cases, it will be necessary to run the plan by an executive-level group for final approval. If this is a requirement, the session should be timed so that executive review and approval can be quickly achieved. Do not schedule the planning session when the executive body will not be available until a month later!

4. Follow up

It is vital to follow up the blitz-build by quickly assembling the actual plan and distributing it for comments and then for rapid publication. The best way to do this is to have a clerical person present at the blitz-build with a laptop computer to record all the important information that goes up on the easel pads. This person can consolidate information as the session moves ahead, and should be willing to work through breaks and meals, even late into the evening, in order to give the participants rapid printouts of the contents of the plan.

As soon as possible, preferably the next day, roll out the plan to the organization and start to implement it. Then start tracking and assessing its effectiveness and set a date for a future off-site meeting to review the progress and update the plan.

What About a Really Big House?

There is no question that you can blitz-build a strategic plan for any of the following organizations in just a day or two, given the proper pre-work and planning:

- Most city or county governments.
- Any company with a single focus, even if it has multiple locations; for example, a tire manufacturer with plants in seven states.
- Any single manufacturing or service site; for example, a large hospital or factory—even up to 7,000 employees.
- Any college or medium sized university.
- Any single state governmental agency.
- Any local, statewide or national voluntary organization that has a single focus.
- Any local church.
- Any single school or school system.

- Any single hospital or healthcare provider.
- Any single agency of local government.

However, there are some organizations that are extremely big and will require a sustained planning effort over several months. Examples would include:

- A state government.
- A large diversified private company.
- A major university.
- A national voluntary organization with multiple missions, such as the American Red Cross.
- A national church organization, such as the Southern Baptist Convention or the Catholic Archdiocese of New York.
- A statewide school system.

These large, complex organizations require more time, not because they are more sophisticated, but because they are often more confused than their smaller cousins. Sears and Roebuck, for example, expanded from a well-focused retail store into a multifaceted company that apparently lacked a common internal sense of mission. They have rebounded by reducing the scope of their enterprise back to a point where they now appear to have a clear sense of mission.

Large organizations often lack a consensus as to what their mission really is. However, a team can still be assembled. Instead of a one- or two-day blitz, the quality manager should plan on a series of one-day meetings, spread out over two to three months to wrestle with each step of the strategic planning process. This allows the team members time to go back to their peers between meetings.

Big may mean confused, but it does not always mean slow. A fast "ready, aim, fire" philosophy is even more important for large organizations. The quality manager and the facilitator need to push the planning process as fast as the organizational culture will allow.

The pre-planning should be conducted on a broader scale as well. If an organization has multiple missions and multiple customers, the planning team needs to be in contact with all the customer types and this can require more time and effort. The team must at least sample the various types of customers to be sure they understand the full range of customer interests.

Working with an organization on this scale, benchmarking (as planning team pre-work) should be conducted on a global scale, because competition at this level is almost always global. Look at what the best governments, businesses, and universities in the world are doing. After all, this is what the Japanese have done consistently since the Meiji Restoration, benchmarking globally to design a system of government patterned after Great Britain, an educational system that draws from Germany, and an economic system patterned after the United States. Just remember that the Japanese did not uncritically mimic other global entities. Instead, they identified effective ideas and incorporated those ideas into their own pattern of behavior.

Refinements

There are some refinements you can add to your blitz-building in order to embellish the process. For instance, you might kick off the process by having the senior manager, or mayor, governor, president, superintendent etc., set the stage for the process by issuing a letter to the team members to invite them to be participants in this process. A thank-you letter at the end is a good idea, too.

The quality manager might want to arrange for a special keepsake memento for the participants, such as a coffee mug, t-shirt, or a formal jacket with the organization's logo.

This will commemorate the activity and reward people for the extra effort that was put forth.

Facilitators

The quality field is now full of all sorts of facilitators. We have quality improvement facilitators, team facilitators, problem-solving facilitators, and facilitators for root cause analysis.

Likewise, there is a plethora of strategic planning consultants. Most universities have business faculty who provide this consulting as a side venture, and there are full-time private consulting firms in this field. What your organization will need is a hybrid; someone who knows the quality discipline and who also understands strategic planning.

An organization can develop this type of staff person internally by taking a strong quality professional, who has demonstrated skill in facilitating teams, and sending him or her to a program on strategic planning, such as those offered at the Owen Graduate School of Management at Vanderbilt University.

Or, you can borrow such a person from another organization through an executive loan program. City and state governments and voluntary organizations can use a local executive from the private sector through a loan-type program. Organizations can also tap into the a federally sponsored programs for retired senior managers who are willing to provide consulting help.

Another option is to hire a facilitator. If you go this route, here are some attributes to seek:

1. Process knowledge—the person knows how to facilitate a group of people and knows strategic thinking.
2. Technical knowledge of the quality field—facilitator needs well-rounded knowledge, and should not be dogmatically attached to a particular guru or method.

3. People skills—must be amiable but able to push the team.
4. Facilitator needs to be willing to take the time to learn the language of your organization and meet your needs without meddling in your affairs, and without trying to get hired into a position in your organization.

This chapter opened with a quote from Mr. Shoichiro Irimajiri of Honda of America, drawing from his five principles of "racing spirit." Part of the winning combination in motor racing, business, government, or any other enterprise is to be ready on time. Organizations often cannot wait for weeks and months to develop and update their strategic plan. The blitz-building process can help the quality manager have a plan in place that provides punctual performance for the organization.

Continuously Improving the Strategic Planning Process

The organization's strategic planning process itself can be continuously improved. The quality manager should ask participants on the planning team how the overall process can be enhanced, and people in the organization should be asked whether or not the plan provides them with a roadmap for organizational change. Other organizations' strategic planning processes should be benchmarked in order to keep improving your own process.

Whether you employ a blitz-build approach or any other method, consider that your strategic planning process has inputs, a process, and outputs. Strive for continuous improvement of the inputs and the process in order to maximize the quality of the outputs. Review the cycle time of the planning process and seek to ensure that your process is both effective and efficient.

Chapter 11

Quality Standards, Award Criteria, Benchmarking, and Philosophies

> "People don't work for companies; they work for people. Those who don't work well or efficiently need a beacon to line themselves up with."
>
> *Philip B. Crosby,* Quality Without Tears

Every quality manager, line manager, and quality professional who uses this book will interpret its contents from his or her own experience and knowledge base, and will seek to apply a strategic planning process that will fit within the unique circumstances of his or her organization. Every organization has its unique history—what it tried in the past, which quality guru it has followed, or what national or international standard it applies. The organization's history has shaped the current situation.

The purpose of this chapter is not to critique any quality standard, award program, or philosophy, but to offer thoughts about how to use this strategic planning process to improve your organization's quality movement from what-

205

ever condition it may be in today. To do so, we need to incorporate various standards, award criteria, and philosophies into the strategic planning.

You Probably Have a Mutt

There are not many organizations that have a quality effort based only on one standard, one guru, or one principle. What you probably have in your organization is a mutt—a polyglot mongrel with all sorts of baggage that must be recognized, enshrined, or laid to rest. The exception to this observation is the organization that has been asleep for the last fifteen years and just woke up to the quality movement last year when some outside group, like its customer, demanded that it adhere to some standard it had never heard of before.

Most organizations that have been investing time and energy in quality have an effort based on a mixed set of premises and practices. Some unfortunate organizations have such a hodgepodge of beliefs that their quality movement is consumed by an internal struggle for visibility and control.

Standards

Many organizations build their quality approach around a consensus standard. Some standards have long histories and focus on a specific industry, such as NQA-1, while others are newer and designed for broad use, such as ISO 9000.

NQA-1 means Nuclear Quality Assurance-1, a consensus standard that was developed for use in the nuclear power industry. This standard outlines the key quality requirements for the design, fabrication, operation, and decommission of a nuclear power station. In this standard, you will find guidance for training, inspection, auditing, drawings, procedures, purchasing, calibration of test equipment, and the establishment of an overall quality program. This standard keeps reactors from having core meltdowns.

ISO 9000 is virtually a watered down version of NQA-1, written so that it can be applied to any industry or service organization. It outlines key requirements for the design, fabrication, and operation of systems that can be subdivided into specific processes. Not much is said about waste and decommissioning. ISO 9000 is written primarily to provide assurance of product and service consistency between organizations in order to minimize the cost of inspecting a vendor's product. Being ISO 9000 certified is a good step in being able to convince customers of the overall quality of your product and the control of variation in your processes.

Of course some industries and government agencies are not satisfied with a national or international standard. The automotive industry, for example, has written their own version of ISO 9000 that they are applying specifically to the manufacture of automotive parts. Likewise, the U.S. Department of Energy has developed its own standard for quality that it applies to nuclear research and weapons development. The Department of Defense has numerous standards (military specifications) that are applied to its contractors. Restaurants will develop their own set of internal standards for control of quality; at the same time they meet quality standards set by government agencies.

So, there are a lot of standards, and if your organization has a quality program that is based on a standard, you are by no means special. Many organizations currently have no strategic plan other than a desire to comply with a specific standard. While compliance to a standard can be a powerful motivator and a step toward achieving great improvements, compliance to a standard by itself does not provide the value of having a strategic plan.

Here are some things to keep in mind about standards:

1. Standards are based on a consensus—they are written by a group of experts who represent the interests of

their industry and their profession. The consensus in a standard is often the lowest common denominator that the experts can agree upon—standards often give broad admonishments, leaving each organization a great deal of flexibility as to how it meets the standard.

2. Standards are oriented toward inspections and audits to verify compliance to the expectations and requirements.

3. Most standards are strong on the traditional quality tools—plans, controls, and verification, and weak on the less traditional quality tools—people involvement, strategic thinking, and continuous improvement.

4. Most standards are weak on the use of quality philosophies, such as Deming's "profound knowledge" or Juran's emphasis on senior management leadership. However, the ISO 9000 standards have more emphasis on process and continuous process-based improvement than earlier, industry-based standards.

5. There is a trend for standards to be rewritten over time to attempt to include newer quality concepts, but the result is often weak. Again using ISO 9000 as an example, the addition of a section on the use of statistical tools is a welcome addition, but appears as an afterthought instead of an integrated concept.

For many organizations, adherence to a standard is a lifesaving event. The standard can force the organization to develop more rigor in planning, procurement, process control, and documentation, making its product viable to customers. The requirement to meet a standard can give the quality manager a valuable fulcrum with which to move the organization.

However, implementation of a standard is an enabling action, or a set of enabling actions, and should not be considered, in and of itself, to be a comprehensive quality strategy.

Since standards deal with the lowest common denominators, they provide their users with the most basic acceptable level of quality, not a world-class system. Organizations that attempt to make a standard their sole basis for a quality effort will not be able to keep up with their competitors who use a standard as a firm foundation on which to expand.

If your organization is pursuing certification to a standard at the moment, do all you can to bring the organization up to meeting the requirements of that standard. Once your organization has met the requirements, then be prepared to propose a strategic planning process to:

- Capitalize on the gains that have been made.
- Stay ahead of the competition.

In other words, stay the course, obtain your certification, and then get ready to develop your strategic plan so you can keep up the momentum. Do not try to develop a strategic plan in the middle of gaining certification to a standard. It will confuse everyone in your organization.

If your organization has already implemented a standard and is meeting the basic requirements, then it is time either to gradually develop a strategic plan, or go for a blitz-build that will sharply focus the organization on what needs to be done next.

As you move from conforming to a standard toward a more proactive strategic planning process, you should build on the successes your organization has achieved by implementing a standards-based quality program. Do not throw out your success and make a radical change in favor of some other approach.

Instead, develop the vision of what you want to become as an organization that embraces quality as a foundation principle (as outlined in Chapters 3 and 4). Look at how your standards-based program meets your mission and vision and identify the gaps between where you want the organization to be in the future and where it is now (as outlined in Chapter 4). Then ask yourself, "Can we close these gaps by improving our current quality program?" For example, "Can we close the gap by expanding our current use of teams, or by a wider use of statistical tools?"

If you find that expanding what you are already doing will not suffice to close the gaps, then you must search for something new by benchmarking or learning a new aspect of the quality discipline. For instance, your organization may decide that adding new tools to the toolbox, like quality function deployment or root cause analysis, can help you close your gaps.

Award Criteria

Most organizations that are basing their quality efforts on an award criteria now look to the Malcolm Baldrige National Quality Award.

Some organizations are fortunate enough to operate in states that have their own state-level quality awards, such as Tennessee and Minnesota, that are Baldrige-based. However, most organizations will look to the national program for guidance as to what an effective quality program can look like.

Like standards, the Baldrige criteria are developed in a consensus manner. The original team included experts from a spectrum of private and governmental perspectives. It is not necessary to apply for an award to use the criteria for assessment purposes.

Where a standard will define the minimal requirements of a quality program, the Baldrige criteria outline how the best quality system might appear. This is why they include broad areas, such as the strategic plan and the utilization of human resources, that are largely ignored in most standards.

Critics will still point out that the award winners can have problems, such as deficiencies in environmental compliance and protection, that new standards (like ISO 14000) address. Other critics have scoffed at the Baldrige as a marketing tool. There is valid criticism of the manner in which a few award winners have touted their award-winning status, but they did, after all, work hard and invest to achieve that status. And, if customers want quality, why not let them know you are the best in delivering quality products and services, based on an impartial evaluation process?

As with standards, there are some organizations who will invent their own award programs, and this is a positive trend. State-level quality awards multiply the effect of the national effort. Governmental agencies, such as the Department of Energy, that have excellent quality programs but are not eligible to compete for the Baldrige, are stimulating their internal quality movement by creating their own quality awards programs. There are numerous award programs for organizations operating in the government sector. The Presidential Award for Quality has recently been developed as a Baldrige-type award for federal organizations. The U.S. Senate offers a Productivity Award for federal agencies. For quality in the environmental field, there is the National Environmental Policy Act Quality Award.

Here are some thoughts to consider when basing your quality efforts on an award program criteria:

1. Award criteria are based on a consensus; they generally encompass a broader range of quality perspectives than most industry-based standards.
2. The relative value of each evaluation criterion may or may not be helpful to your specific organization, but it is important that you do look at all the criteria. So, do not overlook a criterion because it receives only 5

percent of the weighted significance. That 5 percent may address your organization's Achilles heel.

3. It is very important to consider how you will use the award criteria—as a standard to compare against, as a goal to achieve, as an interesting point of view, or as part of an application process.

If your organization has rejected the idea of using award criteria, then you need to regroup. This is like the children of Israel seeing the Promised Land and turning back into the wilderness for another decade. In this situation, the quality manager needs to drive a stake into the ground and use every opportunity he or she has to lobby for creating a strategic plan.

Using Standards and Award Criteria for Assessments

Quality awards, along with industry, national, and international standards, provide a common benefit to organizations in their use as a tool for assessing an organization's quality program and overall performance.

The assessment can be conducted internally, or externally by an evaluator. Both approaches provide constructive feedback as to where the organization currently stands. Using an award or standard as an assessment tool is an excellent method for identifying the gaps that need to be closed.

The distinction between standards and the Baldrige criteria is a distinction between the minimum set of requirements established on a pass or fail basis, and an evaluation against the highest level of potential achievement.

For the purpose of strategic planning, an organization can identify the criteria of a particular standard or an award program as the core of its vision and identify the gaps between its current status and the vision, along with the activities that need to be taken to close the gaps.

Internal assessments can also be made to determine progress toward achieving the organization's vision. An external assessment can be used to prove that the vision has been achieved. Then, it will be time to expand and renew the vision.

Quality Philosophies

Many organizations have made significant progress in improving the quality of their products and processes by adhering closely to the teachings of one or more of the major quality advocates—Crosby, Juran, and Deming. Some organizations have also gotten bogged down in debate over these philosophies and have not made much progress. The following will be helpful if your organization is developing a strategic plan after having worked with any of these philosophies.

From Crosby:

If your managers have attended the Crosby Quality College, then they are starting with a strong, traditional view of quality, assuming they bought in to what was taught. Like the use of a standard, the Crosby approach emphasizes having a plan and doing what your plan calls for. This is a very orderly approach—comfortable for many and confounding to others. Also, like the use of a standard, the Crosby discipline is an enabling action.

As a quality manager, you will want to reinforce Crosby's often overlooked philosophical side, which emphasizes quality as a strategy. Launch your strategic planning process by focusing on the role of quality in the organization's mission. Use your Crosby-based successes as examples of core enabling actions, and then add to them based upon your organization's needs and the expectations of your customers.

From Juran:

If you have built your quality efforts on Juran's tapes and training, then you probably have a strong, management-driven quality council, lots of quality improvement teams, and many success stories.

Having worked with the Juran tapes and training at a facility that was among the first to use them in 1983, and having been a speaker at the Juran Impro Conferences in 1987, 1989, and 1990, I know firsthand the broad strength of the Juran perspective.

An organization that has been using the Juran methods may have already moved on to the Baldrige criteria for its quality philosophy. In any case, a strategic plan will be a helpful way to regroup and renew the quality effort. Over time, the Juran approach works so well that it can become viewed as mundane and needs a spirited revival on occasion.

While Juran emphasizes the role of top management in quality planning, I still contend that the planning team should include middle management and employees, even union leaders, along with the top managers in order to gain the perspective of all the vital stakeholders.

From Deming:

Deming spoke eloquently on the subject of strategic thinking, as we see in his "14 Obligations for Management" and his "Five Deadly Diseases." Unfortunately, many people did not look beyond the immediate issue of control charts to understand his teaching on strategy.

If Deming were here to comment on the development of a strategic plan, he might admonish people to understand their processes, constantly seek to improve, and not to be distracted by fluctuations in the quarterly reports. Deming's message was strategic in its very nature and has been missed by those who were only looking for a new tactic.

If your organization is one of the rare ones that is truly influenced by Deming, then begin your strategic planning process by examining the 14 Obligations and the Five Deadly Diseases as pre-work for your planning team. His teachings should clearly emerge in your statement of mission, vision, and values.

As the quality manager in an organization that has aligned itself with Deming's strategic views, you would do well to continue to use the small group of consultants known as the "Deming disciples" to facilitate your strategic planning process. However, you will also gain a lot by tossing the Baldrige criteria into the pot as an additional perspective for developing your overall strategy.

Many Pathways Up Each Mountain

In the long run, it may not matter where your organization has been so far in its quality journey. Whether you have relied on Deming, ISO 9000, quality circles, quality function deployment, Crosby, control charts, root cause analysis, Juran, or audits, is not what matters.

What matters is where your organization is headed *now* and how you are going to help it get there. In the here and now, organizations must repeatedly take stock of their strengths and weaknesses, adjust their vision, and focus their attention and resources to meet new challenges.

Just remember that there is no one "right" path for all organizations to pursue. As the Chinese proverb says, "There are many mountains up to heaven, and many pathways up each mountain."

Strategic planning is a pathfinding process. Each group will use the process in its own way to discover its own mountain and its own path.

I hope you will be able to use this book as a tool to help your organization find its path up the right mountain.

Bibliography

On the Future and the Past

Bellamy, Edward. *Looking Backward*. New York: Magnum Books Reprint, 1888.

Downs, Ray F. *Japan Yesterday and Today*. London: Praeger Publishers, 1970.

Kahn, Herman. *Things to Come*. New York: MacMillan, 1972.

————. *The Next 200 Years*. New York: William Morrow & Co., 1976.

————. *The Coming Boom*. New York: Simon & Schuster, 1982.

McHale, John. *The Future of the Future*. New York: Ballantine, 1969.

Naisbitt, John. *Megatrends*. New York: Warner Books, 1982.

————. *Global Paradox*. New York: Avon Books, 1994.

Theobold, Robert. *Teg's 1994*. Chicago: Swallow Press, 1972.

Toynbee, Arnold. *A Study of History*. London: Oxford University Press, 1954.

On Education

Bradley, Leo. *Total Quality Management for Schools*. Lancaster: On Purpose Associates, 1993.

Brookfield, Stephen. *Developing Critical Thinkers*. San Francisco: Jossey-Bass, 1990.

Freire, Paulo. *The Politics of Education*. South Hadley: Bergin & Garvey, 1985.

Mezirow, Jack. *Fostering Critical Reflection in Adulthood*. San Francisco: Jossey-Bass, 1990.

Neuroth, Joann et. al. *TQM Handbook: Applying the Baldrige Criteria to Schools*. Lansing: On Purpose Associates, 1992.

Schon, Donald. *The Reflective Practitioner*. New York: Basic Books, 1983.

Shor, Ira. *Empowering Education*. Chicago: University of Chicago Press, 1992.

Smialek, Mary Ann. "Total Quality in K-12 Eduction." *Quality Progress* (May 1995), pp. 69–72.

On Facilitating

Auvine, Brian et. al. *A Manual for Group Facilitators*. Madison: Center for Conflict Resolution, 1977.

Avery, Michel et. al. *Building United Judgment*. Madison: Center for Conflict Resolution, 1981.

Bradford, Leland. "Leading the Large Meeting." *Adult Education Bulletin* (December 1949), pp. 38–50.

Converse, Joan et. al. *Survey Questions*. Newbury Park: Sage Publications, 1986.

Gantt, Henry. *Industrial Leadership*. New Haven: Yale University Press, 1916.

Heron, John. *The Facilitator's Handbook*. London: Kogan Page, 1989.

Janis, Irving. *Victims of Groupthink*. Boston: Houghton Mifflin, 1972.

Kepner-Tregoe. *Process Consulting.* Princeton: Princeton Research Press, 1976.

Klein, Alan. *Effective Groupwork.* New York: Association Press, 1972.

Knowles, Malcolm, and Knowles, Hulda. *Introduction to Group Dynamics.* New York: Cambridge, 1972.

Lippitt, Gordon. *Individuality and Teamwork.* Washington D.C.: Leadership Resources, 1964.

London, Manuel. *Change Agents.* San Francisco: Jossey-Bass, 1990.

Mills, Theodore. *The Sociology of Small Groups.* Englewood Cliffs: Prentice-Hall, 1967.

Mosley, Donald C. "Nominal Grouping As an Organizational Development Intervention Technique." *Training and Development Journal* (March 1974), pp. 30–37.

Parry, Scott. *From Managing to Empowering.* New York: Quality Resources, 1994.

On Management

Covey, Stephen R. *The Seven Habits of Highly Effective People.* New York: Simon & Schuster, 1989.

Emery, Fred, and Throrsrud, Einar. *Democracy at Work.* Leiden: Martinus Mijhoff, 1976.

Ewen, Ann J. "Enhancing Performance Appraisals with 360 degree Feedback" *Proceedings of the 23rd Annual National Energy & Environmental Symposium.* Milwaukee: ASAC, 1996.

Hammer, Mike, and Champy, J. *Reengineering The Corporation: A Manifesto for Revolution.* New York: Harper Business, 1993.

Kepner, Charles, and Tregoe, Benjamin. *The New Rational Manager.* Princeton: Princeton Research Press, 1981.

Koch, Lester, and French, John. "Overcoming Resistance to Change." *Human Relations* (1948), pp. 512–532.

Kouzes, James, and Posner, Barry. *The Leadership Challenge.* San Francisco: Jossey-Bass, 1987.

Likert, Rensis. *New Patterns of Management.* New York: McGraw-Hill, 1961.

Miller, Lawrence M. *Barbarians to Bureaucrats.* New York: Clarkson N. Potter, Inc., 1989.

Peters, Thomas, and Waterman, Robert. *In Search of Excellence.* New York: Warner Communications, 1982.

Thomas, Kenneth W., and Thomas, Gail Fann. *Power Base Inventory.* Tuxedo, N.Y.: XICOM, 1991.

Tregoe, Benjamin, and Zimmerman, John. *Top Management Strategy.* New York: Simon & Schuster, 1980.

Trist, Eric. *Organizational Change.* London: Tavistock Press, 1963.

Weisbord, Marvin. *Productive Workplaces.* San Francisco: Jossey-Bass, 1987.

On Quality

AT&T. *A Summary of the AT&T Universal Card Services Malcolm Baldrge National Quality Award Application.* Schaumburg: Quality and Productivity Management Association, 1993.

American National Standard. *QS-9000-1-1994.* Milwaukee: ASQC, 1994.

Appleman, Kaye, and Large, Kris. "Navy Hospital Fights Disease With A Quality Team." *Quality Progress* (1995).

Buch, Kimberly, and Shelnutt, J. William, "UNC Charlotte Measures the Effects of Its Quality Initiative." *Quality Progress* (1995).

Butz, Howard E. "Strategic Planning: The Missing Link in TQM." *Quality Progress.* 1995.

Cadillac. *Cadillac: The Quality Story.* Detroit: Cadillac Motor Company, 1991.

Camp, Robert C. *Benchmarking: The Search for Industry Best Practices that Lead to Superior Performance.* New York: Quality Resources, 1989.

Cap, Frank. "The Continuing Quest for Excellence." *Quality Progress* (1995).

Crosby, Philip B. *Quality Is Free.* New York: New American Library, 1979.

———. *Quality Without Tears.* New York: McGraw-Hill, 1984.

Deming, W. Edwards. *Quality, Productivity, and Competitive Position.* Boston: Massachusetts Institute of Technology, 1982.

———. *Out of the Crisis.* Boston: Massachusetts Institute of Technology, 1982.

Ermer, Donald S. "Using QFD Becomes and Educational Experience for Students and Faculty." *Quality Progress* (1995).

Fendt, Paul et. al. *Quality Improvement in Continuing Higher Education and Service Organizations.* Lewiston: Edwin Mellen Press, 1992.

Gada, Ken W. and Oakland, John S. "Chimera or Culture? Business Process Reengineering for Total Quality Management." *Quality Management Journal* 3, no. 3 (1996).

Holoviak, Stephen J. "Negative Attitudes and Quality Circles" *Quality Digest,* 1989. 79–83.

Imai, M. *Kaizen: The Key to Japan's Competitive Success.* New York: McGraw-Hill, 1986.

Ishikawa, Kaoru. *Guide to Quality Control.* Tokyo: Asian Productivity Organization (distributed by Quality Resources), 1976.

Juran, Joseph M. *Managerial Breakthrough.* New York: McGraw-Hill, 1964.

———. *Juran on Leadership for Quality.* New York: Free Press, 1989.

McDermott, Robin E. et. al. *Employee Driven Quality.* New York: Quality Resources, 1993.

Palermo, Richard C., ed. *A World of Quality: Business Transformation at Xerox.* Burr Ridge, Ill.: Business One Irvin, 1993.

Rubach, Laura, and Stratton, Brad. "Mixing Mediums Is the Message." *Quality Progress* (1995).

Schultz, Louis E. *Profiles in Quality.* New York: Quality Resources, 1994.

Shewhart, W. A. *Economic Control of Quality of Manufactured Product.* New York: Van Nostrand, 1931.

Smith, Sheila J. "Blue Cross/Blue Shield of Ohio: A Profile in Change." *Quality Progress* (1995).

Wallace Company. *A Condensed Version of the Company's Application for the Award.* Houston: American Productivity and Quality Center, 1991.

Index

223